Denise

Keep Soaking

Dr S Clark

Pray & Grow Richer

Pray & Grow Richer

Dr. Shirley K. Clark

Pray & Grow Richer
Copyright © 2013
Dr. Shirley K. Clark
Shirley Clark International Ministries

Printed in the United States of America

ISBN 978-0692378465

Published by:
Jabez Books Writers' Agency
(A Division of Clark's Consultant Group)
www.clarksconsultantgroup.com

Cover picture taken by Kauwuane Burton

1. Prayer & Intercession 2. Personal Finance 3. Christian Living

Endorsements

Pray & Grow Richer is a vital book for today's Christians. Helping the Body of Christ break out of a poverty mindset and shift into Kingdom understanding has been a challenge. Dr. Shirley Clark draws revelation concerning this challenge from her experiences in life. She tackles this great task with a depth of understanding from the Word of God. Dr. Clark stresses the necessity of prayer to receive revelation from God for financial blessings.

Reading and implementing the practical steps in this book will change your future. You will be propelled into your destiny as a Christian entrepreneur. I highly recommend *Pray & Grow Richer* for every believer.

Barbara Wentroble
Founder, International Breakthrough Ministries
Founder, Business Owners for Christ International
Certified Life Coach
CEO of Breakthrough Business Network
Coppell, TX

Dr. Shirley Clark is a woman who honors God and honors the Word. You will be blessed by her book, ***Pray and Grow Richer***.

Dr. Nasir Siddiki
Best-Selling Author/Entrepreneur
Founder, Wisdom Ministries
Tulsa, OK

Dr. Clark has penned a masterpiece about how marketplace ministry and soaking prayers can work together to increase your personal wealth. *Pray & Grow Richer* is a must read, and I highly recommend it to every Christian who wants to do great things for God.

Dr. Keith Johnson
America's #1 Confidence Coach
Spring Hill, FL

Once again, Dr. Shirley, the Prayer Strategist, has shown us how to position and posture ourselves in prayer to receive strategy from God Almighty in order to receive what God has for us. She shows us how through absolute faith in God we can petition God in prayer, and receive divine strategy on how to live an abundant life. It's time for us to increase in our wealth, spiritually, physically and financially, and this is an incredible tool that will show you the practical steps to implement in your life to begin living an empowered life now!

Pastor Renee Hornbuckle
Senior Pastor, Agape Church
Arlington, TX

It is rare that you find a practical tool that helps you merge your faith with the results that you desire. Dr. Shirley Clark's book, *Pray and Grow Richer,* is just that masterpiece that will empower you to dig deeper and produce the results that you desire. This is a must read for every person of prayer!

Apostle Tyrone Lister
Author & Entrepreneur
Circle of Influence, CEO/Founder
Frisco, TX

Dr. Shirley has done a masterful job on this well timed manuscript. She is one of today's upcoming kingdom millionaires for the season ahead. I believe Dr. Shirley has hit the mark in transforming the common mind-set from Church Mentality to Kingdom Mentality. After reading and studying the pages you're holding in yours hands, you, too, will shift from a menu mentality to now taking your seat at the table mentality. Well done my sister, let the shift begin!

Apostle Christopher J. Hardy
International Covenant Life Network
International Covenant Connect
Plano, TX

Dedication

This book is dedicated to Pastor Suzette Caldwell, Co-Pastor of Windsor Village United Methodist Church in Houston, TX. It was upon meeting this woman of God that I fully understand the meaning of how to *Pray and Grow Richer*. It was in 2008 that God allowed me to meet Pastor Suzette Caldwell in Dallas, TX at a Women's Conference. I had heard her name about six or seven years before, and that she taught on prayer, but that was the extent of my knowing. So at this conference, she was teaching on prayer as well.

As I attended her session, I noticed on her brochure, she had a Prayer Institute. This piqued my interest, so I asked if my assistant and I could come and visit her Prayer Institute. She gave us permission to come and in about two months, we were able to fit it into our schedule to visit the Institute. Boy, were we shocked!

Within five minutes being on their campus, I knew God had set us up. We had no idea that Pastor Suzette and her church owned a mall along with numerous facilities, schools, and businesses we toured that day. But the most amazing thing was the strategy that they used to acquire most of this. What was this strategy – PRAYER!

You see, Pastor Suzette and her incredible leadership team in their Supernatural Communications Department had tapped into a win-win model for the church to *Pray and Grow Richer.* They understood in order for the kingdom of God to be advanced in a tremendous capacity, they would have to implement and activate prayer strategies that birthed in what they needed in the spirit first before it was manifested in the natural.

How did they do this? They have a team of anointed marketplace ministry scribers that prays and seeks God religiously for the growth and development of all strategic plans for their church. And after they have sought God for about two weeks to 30 days, they write out the prayers that the Holy Spirit unction them to write, then they put them in a monthly booklet and distribute them to every household in their church to bring the entire church on one accord in believing for a certain need or vision of the pastor, church and/or members. Because they have mastered this oneness endeavor in fortifying a congregation to pray in unison, they acquire property, land, businesses, etc. at an accelerated rate. This team led by Pastor Suzette Caldwell is incredible!

Kudos, to you, Pastor Suzette Caldwell! My life was never the same after meeting you. I can't thank God enough for you. Love you, dearly! I am a true living epistle of your impact and influence.

Acknowledgements

- I would like to thank the Lord for always being my comforter, guide, and help throughout my life in Him.

- A special thank you to my husband, Thurman Clark, and my children: Danielle & Quinton, for allowing me to be all that God has called me to be.

- As well, I would like to especially thank my pastors of 17 years, Bishop Thomas Dexter Jakes and First Lady Serita Jakes. It has been the entrepreneur and writer's anointing upon their lives that have inspired, impacted and cajoled my life that as of now, I have written over 20 books and own a consultant business with six major departments: Publication, Leadership Institute, Event Planning, Public Relations & Marketing, Entertainment & Speaker's Bureau, and Coaching & Corporate Training.

- Lastly, I would like to thank Patricia Scott, April Quick and Kenesia Mouton that assisted me in the final development of this manuscript. Thank you for lending your time and talent to me.

Disclaimer

Dr. Shirley Clark and/or Shirley Clark International Ministries do not purport to be a Financial Advisor or any type of financial consultant. The information in this book about finances has been shared solely for the purpose for information, inspiration and encouragement. Dr. Shirley Clark and/or Shirley Clark International Ministries encourage everyone who read this book to seek financial advice from a trained professional before making any changes to their financial situation recommended in this book.

Table of Contents

From Frustration to Favor

"Thou shalt arise, and have mercy upon Zion: for the time to favour her, yea, the set time, is come."

Psalm 102:13

Wow...**Pray & Grow Richer.** The day that I heard these words in my spirit, I said wow -- this is awesome! Then I got even more excited. I said to myself, "I am going to write a book called, **Pray & Grow Richer."** But it wasn't too long after this that I began to feel an uneasiness within me. I felt slightly weird; then all of a sudden an extreme unsettledness began to erupt inside of me.

Our history is always a catalyst for our current state of being and whether we like it or not, it is a voice of the choices we have made in our past or grew up in.

As I pondered on this awkwardness that I was feeling for a few minutes, I finally realized what I was encountering. I was dealing with a religious spirit. And this spirit began to say to me, "How can you have the audacity to link prayer and prosperity together like this? Have you lost your mind? You will be scorned in the religious arena."

For a brief moment, I lent my ears to these sayings, and I almost abandoned this idea. Then I realized this is the kind of spirit that has kept most of God's people broke and in despair for many years – a religious spirit. And yes, I am well aware that just the title of this book might sound sacrilegious, but before you write me off, let me encourage you to give this book a chance and continue to read. It is never my desire to foster a teaching in the body of Christ that will bring a "black" mark on the kingdom of God. Rather, it is my heart to reveal my experiences that have brought me to the place that I am now writing this type of resource tool to glorify Him. Our history is always a catalyst for our current state of being and whether we like it or not, it is a voice of the choices we have made in our past or grew up in. So I am taking a chance, going ahead, to write this book, and perhaps, there is at least one person in the body of Christ tired of being broke.

I, like many in America was raised in poverty. With no guide or mentor to get me out of my situation; therefore, being reared in such a negative environment marred and warped my thinking, behavior and life. This is why I cannot believe a child who was brought up in poverty truly wanted to be nurtured in this type of environment. So what I do believe and know is that poverty is a trap and if there is no *long-term* intervention, it enslaves people that are brought up within these settings.

For years, as a child, I was angry at my livelihood and the lifestyle I was subjected to, but I was not empowered to change it. So I became bitter at my parents for bringing me up in such an impoverished environment. Much of this frustration was fostered because some of the kids at school sometimes would make fun of what I wore. What can you say when you know what they are saying is true, but you don't have the power to change the situation? It was what it was. And for me, it felt like a lifetime.

> *What most people fail to understand is that in order to break a poverty mentality out of someone's life that has been exposed to negativity all their life will require not just a brief period of intervention, but consistent interaction with a mediator (not a mentor).*

How does a child recover from these types of situations and environments? Well, it will take some type of *protracted* intervention that allows room for mistakes to be made, and someone leading the way that understands this and will continue to believe in you. What do I mean? Many people that are well off or have a better quality of life when they reach back to assist someone that was raised in conditions such as I was, for some reason want us to begin to make better decisions within a short span of time. And when we don't, they give up on us and say we will never amount to anything.

What most people fail to understand is that in order to break a poverty mentality out of someone's life that has been exposed to negativity all their life will require not just a brief period of intervention, but consistent interaction with a mediator (not a mentor) that will walk with them and provide opportunities for them to grow over an extended period of time. This is what I needed. However, I never got it.

What do you do when there is no one willing to be your mediator?

I am glad you asked. That is why I am writing this book. Yes, I have plenty of coaches, mentors, and spiritual advisors now, but it was after I was delivered out of my impoverished condition, and many years later, that most of these people came into my life. So what did I do that brought about the change in my life that qualifies me to speak into your life through this book, *"Pray & Grow Richer?"*

Again, I am glad you asked.

It was in 1977, the year that I graduated from high school that I found myself standing at an altar in a medium-small church in Durham, NC, with my sister beside me giving my heart to the Lord. I was not quite sure what I was doing, but the pastor asked for those who wanted to make a change in their lives to come to the altar. He said that Jesus will help us and that we needed a Savior. Again, I was not sure what all of this meant, being that I was only 18 years old, but one thing I knew, I wanted a change in my life. So that day, in church, we gave our lives to the Lord.

Immediately, my sister and I became students of the Word. We changed everything. Everything we were told to do or read in the Bible; we did it. We later found out that some of the things we were told to do were just traditions of men and/or part of a denomination's belief. But the thing that was so real in our hearts was that the way to change was becoming an obedient servant to the Word, which would eventually foster a manifestation of Truth in our lives. Bottom line: There was a promise and expectation that our current situation would change and it would be for the better.

Now, 35 years later (2013), we can truly say that the Word works -- so many in the body of Christ have spent their lives confessing the Word, but never possessing the promises of God. Yes, off and on, they have received sporadic blessings that have *reaffirmed* their confession that God is good; but they have never reached a place in God that allowed their spirits and hearts to *rest* in the blessings of God in the fullness of its potential in their lives.

I am now 53 years old and I can truly say; this place of rest is obtainable. I remember the morning I woke up and said, "I can do what I want to do with my life today." If I want to stay in bed all day, I can. If I want to do something else, I can. It is called the power of choice or the power to have options.

No blessing in the Word of God is automatic. Therefore, we must exercise our faith to receive them.

How does an impoverished young girl move from being a "nobody" to being a desired object of many leaders wanting her to be on their boards? Answer – **PRAYER!** It was what I learned about prayer and its activation in my life that brought me to my current state. No, I did not have a rich uncle or someone left me an inheritance, I just decided to activate that which I said I believe.

In the book of Ephesians, chapter 3: 20 it says, *"Now unto him that is able to do exceeding abundantly above all that we ask or think, according to the power that worketh in us."* The key part of this verse is "worketh in us." I needed God to work some things out of me and in me. How do you dislodge erroneous thinking, replace it with Truth? This is what my sister and I had to do. So, we "devoured" the Word of God.

Next, we activated the Word. .We confessed what we read and believed God above our circumstances. We said, "What did we have to lose?" We were already broke, so we could at least try the Word and see if it would work. Then we asked for what we wanted.

*Now unto him that is able to do exceeding abundantly above all that we ask or think …*whether your thinking is "small" or "big," God can exceed your current condition. We often look at this scripture from a poverty mindset, but no matter what status you are in, God can still exceed your expectations. But for me, because of my upbringing, I did not always know what to ask for. Mentally and emotionally, I was so busy fighting my past, trying to overcome it, that my thinking truly was "small." As I grew in Christ, and my standard of living began to change for the better, my thinking changed as well. Even now as I look back over my life, God was always doing things exceedingly, abundantly above that which I could ask or think. For example:

- I asked God for a good used car and He gave me a new car.

- I asked God to help me write a book, and He gave me a Writers' Agency.

- I asked God for a business, and He gave me five streams of income.

- I asked God to give me a millionaire coach; He gave me several millionaire coaches.

- I asked God to double my income, instead He tripled it.

Gloria Copeland, one of God's leading voices in the 21st Century today says this, *"No blessing in the Word of God is automatic. Therefore, we must exercise our faith to receive them."* This is what we did consistently.

It is through faith and patience we receive the promises of God – *"That ye be not slothful, but followers of them who through faith and patience inherit the promises"* *(Hebrews 6:12).*

As we pressed into the things of God, believing Him for change, we knew revelation stood between us and poverty. The book of James says if any man lack wisdom, let him ask of God (1:5); and I did a lot of asking. It has been 35 years since I received Christ in my life and it was the "revealed" Christ within my life that has brought me to the place that I am in now. It was the relevant, revelatory "Word" being activated in my life over these 35 years that has brought me the victory thus far. God has a covenant determination to prosper His people. Our responsibility is to believe it and receive it.

> *As we pressed into the things of God believing Him for change, we knew revelation stood between us and poverty.*

Because I believe this, He is constantly favoring my life.

⁵For his anger lasts only a moment, but his favor lasts a lifetime; weeping may stay for the night, but rejoicing comes in the morning. "2021"

⁶ When I felt secure, I said, "I will never be shaken."

⁷ LORD, when you favored me, you made my royal mountain stand firm; but when you hid your face, I was dismayed.

⁸ To you, LORD, I called; to the Lord I cried for mercy:

⁹ "What is gained if I am silenced, if I go down to the pit? Will the dust praise you? Will it proclaim your faithfulness?

¹⁰ Hear, LORD, and be merciful to me; LORD, be my help."

¹¹ You turned my wailing into dancing; you removed my sackcloth and clothed me with joy,

¹² that my heart may sing your praises and not be silent. LORD my God, I will praise you forever.

Psalm 30:5-12

God has truly turned my mourning into dancing. I have extreme peace in my life now. While I don't have everything I want, I am beyond being happy. I live a **FULFILLED** life! *Leviticus 26:9 says in the Amplified Version, "For I will be **leaning toward you with favor and regard for you,** rendering you fruitful, multiplying you, and establishing and ratifying My covenant with you."*

God is relentlessly leaning toward me with favor. I receive, confess and believe this word every day. Therefore, everywhere I go, I expect people to favor me.

Psalm 44:3 also says, *"For they got not the land in possession by their own sword, neither did their own arm save them: but thy right hand, and thine arm, and the light of thy countenance, **because thou hadst a favour unto them."***

Whatever I own today, it has been by the grace of God favoring my life. Truly, it was not by my doing, it was the hand of God performing His Word in my life. Every day is the day of God's favor upon my life…*"The Spirit of the Lord is upon me…."*

Say this with me, ***"The Favor of God Is Working On My Behalf Today!***

You have to believe this more than your present circumstances, and then you will begin to see changes in your life.

Chapter Two

The Empowered Mind

"A wise man will hear, and will increase learning; and a man of understanding shall attain unto wise counsels."

Proverbs 1:5

F rom time to time, I have been asked what has been the "thing" that has been a defining moment in my life. If I was to look back over my life and all that God had done for me, what would be that "thing" that marks or stands out in my life that has brought me to my present state? Initially, years ago as people began to ask me this question, I would vacillate between two or three things. But now, as I have gotten older and able to properly assess my life better, I realize the thing that put me on the path that led me to my current state was *reading.* As some say often, it was my Ah-ha moment and others might say it was an epiphany. But, however, it is classified; it was the moment God showed me how important it was to start reading.

It was in 1982, that I was hired to be a substitute in a library system in North Carolina. Soon afterward, a position came open in the billing department and I was hired to supervise this department. This department was a part of the Circulation Department, so I had to work the Circulation Desk daily. I worked at the main branch, so we were very busy.

During those years, we were checking out about 20,000 books a month to patrons, amongst the other items available for check out – videos, magazines, tapes, etc. I was quite good at my job and for the most part enjoyed my co-workers. It was not a match made in heaven, but it was a decent job. Didn't pay much, but it did meet *some* of my needs. But about three or four years into this job, God interrupted my life one day and spoke to my spirit and said, "Why do you think all these people are checking out all of these books? If they are checking out this many books a month, then there must be something to books."

> *World changers are readers. And readers are leaders.*

Immediately, I knew God had spoken something profound in my spirit, and it was the turning point in my life. If all the "lights were out" regarding this before, then they all came on, after He spoke this into my spirit.

I began checking out 25 to 30 books at a time. I checked out and read books on all types of subjects -- from self-help to organizing, from finance to fiction, from cooking to psychology. It did not matter. There was a hunger and thirst that were elicited within me to read books that I could not fulfill. It was an unquenchable thirst.

I tried to drive and read. Every moment in between my personal devotion time, and doing things I really had to do, you could find me reading. The things I learned from books were incredible. Now, I am an avid reader and an advocate for lifelong learning. I try to read or learn something new every day. It is said that in five years you will be the same person except for the CDs you listen to, the DVDs you watch and books you read. If you want your world to change, you have to start reading TODAY!

World changers are readers. And readers are leaders. It is also said:

"If you read 30 to 60 minutes a day in a subject of your choice, after three years you will be known in your community, five years you will be known across the country, and after seven years, you will have worldwide recognition."

One day while I was listening to a CD by a multimillionaire he gave these statistics about how little people read. He said:

- 78% of the people in our society do not go to bookstores

- 90% of the people in our society, do not own a library card

- And most adults after college never read a full book again

- And 90% of most people, died dead broke

These statistics were startling to me. When I heard these statistics initially, I said to myself, how can this be? 78% of the people in our society do not go to bookstores; 90% of the people in our society, do not own a library card, and most adults after college, never read a full book again. These statistics cannot be correct, so I decided to do my own research.

Here are some more definitive statistics I found:

- 1/3 of high school graduates never read another book for the rest of their lives.

- 42 percent of college graduates never read another book after college.

- 80 percent of U.S. families did not buy or read a book last year.

- 70 percent of U.S. adults have not been in a bookstore in the last five years.

- 57 percent of new books are not read to completion.

(Source: Jenkins Group)
http://mentalfloss.com/article/27590/who-reads-books#ixzz2PDRNMSE2

I could not believe what I was reading. For some reason, I thought everybody read some type of publication whether it was a newspaper, magazine or book. I thought I was the only one years ago that was outside of the "club." I thought I was the only one that did not have a "clue." But I see, I am not, and this disturbs me greatly.

Listen, if you are in the body of Christ today and you are not a reader, you need to stop what you are doing and pray and ask God to give you the passion and the desire to read. Reading is extremely important to your mental, physical, emotional and **financial** make up. According to Myron Golden in his book, *From Trash Man to Cash Man,* "Rich people educate themselves and poor people entertain themselves." This statement alone should provoke you to read if you are not a reader.

> *It does matter what you read. You can't read doom and gloom material all the time and expect to have a positive and great outlook on life.*

Reading provides greater avenues or more opportunities for God to expand you ministry sphere and financial portfolio.

Reading brings about expansion and expansion brings about exposure.

Let's give God something *more* to work with.

Now, just so I can cover all the bases, let me say this; it does matter what you read. You can't read doom and gloom material all the time and expect to have a positive and great outlook on life. You have to read uplifting, informative, self-help information. Information, books and publications that will build up your inner man and reinforce a can do attitude. So you want to minimize the doom and gloom information you allow to come into your ear and eye gate. To be perfectly honest, I have found if I don't watch the news for weeks or a month, it will be repeated on some other broadcast or news talk show. I have lived long enough to figure this out.

My life is such a testimony of the goodness of God in this area. God really does have a sense of humor. He has taken a woman who did not know how to correctly write a sentence as well as was not a reader to now owning a Writers Agency. Not only do I own this Agency, but now I am an author of over 17 books and publications. In addition, I also ghostwrite books for other leaders and authors. God is truly able to do exceedingly, abundantly above all we can ask or think.

Dismantling the Poverty Mentality

As I stated in the previous chapter, I was reared in an impoverished environment. And in environments like these, there are certain tenets that are often associated with these lifestyles. One of the biggest is the lack of people pursuing formal education and definitely higher education. This was true in my family.

Both my mother and father had little formal education. My parents got married when they were 16 years old, and they were from the "country." The norm for the natives there was to work the tobacco and corn fields, so getting a formal education was low on their radar. Nor did they have a real visual image to provoke them to change their situation. Yes, there was a public school system, but getting married so young precluded them from pursuing their education. As well, my mother got pregnant soon after they married, so this complicated things even more.

While my siblings and I (there were seven of us) went to school, our main focus was surviving. I was the youngest and much of what my older siblings experienced and knew were not a part of my memory. I was too young to comprehend or remember. But at the age of five, my mother and father separated. Needless to say, this was a very difficult time for my family.

> *One of the greatest barriers poor people have to overcome is the poverty mentality. We can be saved and still be enslaved to our past.*

My father was a functional alcoholic; and from time to time, by my understanding, he would be abusive to my mother. It got to the point, she had to leave him. Can you imagine how difficult this was for her -- a mother of seven children, with little education, where would she find a job to sustain her livelihood? Eventually, she did find a job working as a cook making minimum wages.

Oh, how I remember this time in my life. Lack was a constant companion of my family. My mama would cook a whole box of rice or a whole bag of beans just to have food on the table for us to eat. She wanted so badly to take care of her children.

She never wanted to live in the "project." She just wanted something a little better for her children. But no matter how hard she tried, we were always short on something. To have all of our utilities on at the same time was a blessing. But from time to time, our water or lights would be off. But my mother would work something out to get it cut back on as soon as possible. My mother was truly a stalwart.

It is not enough to have the Truth, but if you don't rid your life of all the offspring of past failures in your life, then you will build your life with these negative offspring influencing it.

She was a Christian all of my life and loved God with all her heart. But where was God during these challenging times? He was always there and from time to time, we would witness her getting an unexpected blessing. But when I got saved, and got under some strong teaching of the

Word, I realized many times my mother went without was because of a poverty mentality.

One of the greatest barriers poor people have to overcome is the poverty mentality. We can be saved and still be enslaved to our past. My mother was a prime example of this. Every time my sister and I would reach back to give my mother some finer things in life after we got saved, she would still eventually wind up operating her life from a poverty mentality. It was a perpetual mental trap that she has never gotten out of even with Jesus in her life.

You see, it is not enough to have the Truth, but if you don't rid your life of all the offspring of past failures in your life, then you will build your life with these negative offspring influencing it. And the sad thing about saints like my mother, they don't know they are operating out of this poverty mentality.

This is one of the main problems with a poverty mentality; it keeps people in a cycle of making poor choices and inadvertently enslaves them to money from an insufficient and lack standpoint. They are always "counting pennies." Because of this, the human heart becomes afflicted and the progeny of such affliction is a perpetual poverty lifestyle.

A poverty mentality is an attitude. It is a way of thinking that is said to precipitate poverty because the focus is on what you do **not** have rather than what you do have. For example comments like: "I can't afford this..." and "I'll never have enough money for that...." Basically, this is an attitude of self-belief and empowerment rather than one of self-pity and jealousy that is thought to combat the destructive poverty mentality.

If we don't want to live in poverty, no matter how much we may wish to be rich or richer, it isn't enough. However, the first step in overcoming the poverty mentality is becoming aware that you have one. So rather than concentrating on what we don't have, we need to focus on what we do have, what our purpose is and how we can positively get what we want.

The Final Conclusion: If you want to see change in your life and your finances, you have to change your **psychology (belief system)** – your way of thinking.

Having a problem with this statement? Well, think about this. If your thinking has gotten you where you are today, then are you really satisfied with your current situation?

If not, will you allow yourself to be teachable, so that this book can revolutionize your life? My promise to you is that I will back everything up with the Word of God.

Immerse Yourself in the Word

Complete immersion in the Word of God is the best starting point to cleansing your mind of erroneous thoughts and thinking. You need to make up in your mind that you are ready for change and you will do whatever it takes to make this change happen. And know for a surety God has given to us everything that pertains to life and godliness.

> *Increase comes with an application attached to it called learning – a wise man will hear and will increase learning.*

2 Peter 1:3, *"According as his divine power hath given unto us all things that pertain unto life and godliness, through the knowledge of him that hath called us to glory and virtue."*

Through the knowledge of him – We must educate ourselves continually with the Truth from God's Word. Remember, the opening scripture for this chapter. *"A wise man will hear, and will increase learning* – you see, it is all about *"increasing."* Many of us want increase in our influence, impact and finances, but we won't do the thing that will bring about increase, and that is expanding our mind – increasing our knowledge base.

Increase comes with an application attached to it called learning – *a wise man will hear and will increase learning.*

There is no way around it. Think about it. Basically, people are **not** hired for employment based on what they do **not** know, but based on what they **do** know and their skill sets. Information is powerful, and it can also be used as a segue into you having great influence.

> *Every Success is not good, **nor** GODLY!!!...God wants us to have good success – success that glorifies Him and His kingdom.*

We are told in Joshua 1:8 that we are to meditate on the Word day and night -- *"This Book of the Law shall not depart from your mouth, but you shall meditate in it day and night, that you may observe to do according to all that is written in it. For then you will make your way prosperous, and then you will have good success."*

Why does God want us to meditate on His Word -- so that we might have good success? We will be talking about this more in the next chapter. But every success is not good, **nor** GODLY!!!! Can the church say, AMEN!!!!

How many times have we heard of people succeeding in life or making it "big" and eventually their success turns into a haven of hell, too many times?

God wants us to have good success -- success that glorifies Him and His kingdom.

Transformational Materials

If you are serious about changing your situation, below is a list of some transformational materials you can read. I advise you to read all of them.

These publications will transform your mind. They will give you what you need to start your mind shifting in the right direction for increase.

In fact, you want to add all of these tools to your financial and faith library. But let me help you out here. Just in case you cannot afford to buy some of these publications right now, you can find some of these materials at your local public library. So don't get discouraged, just be creative.

Also, check on Amazon.com. Sometimes, I have gotten publications for only $.99 cents for used copies. I paid more for the shipping than the book. Regardless, the total cost was under $5 dollar.

As well, there are a lot of books now you can read through purchasing them through kindle. The cost for many of these books is $.99 cents to $5.99. There are myriads of ways to get what you want.

In addition, don't forget about the bloggers. There are a lot of financial advisors and consultants blogging these days. I have folders of downloaded articles written by bloggers. Also, you might want to get on some of these people's websites. When I have read a book by a certain author and I was really blessed by it, I will visit their website and if it piques my interest, I subscribe to their newsletters, updates, training, etc. or join their mailing list. Know some of this might be seasonal, but right now I need what they have. And when I feel I have received all that I need from this person or organization, I unsubscribe.

Listen, I believe the old proverb, "When the student is ready, the teacher will appear." Meaning, when you are serious about your change, then God will come into the situation and help create what you need or provide an avenue for you to connect with whomever you need to complete a task.

It is not magic, it is just a principle. I heard one millionaire say, that if it does not work, then it is not a principle. But if it does work, it is a principle.

Reading or being well read is a principle because it expands your mind and causes growth and increase to come into your life. You can NEVER lose elevating your mind with good "soil."

Here is the list:

- From Trash Man to Cash Man

- One Minute Millionaire

- Secrets of a Millionaire Mind

- The Science of Getting Rich

 Millionaire Maker

- Start Late, Finish Rich

- Retire Young, Retire Rich

- Zero Debt

- Financial Peace

- Rich and Happy

- Why We want You to Be Rich

- Dare to Be Rich

- Think and Grow Rich

- The Road to Wealth

- 9 Steps to Financial Freedom

- The Guide to Becoming Rich

- Law of Attraction

- The Purpose of Prosperity

- The Next Millionaire

- The Millionaire Next Door

- Rich Dad, Poor Dad

Here are some of the covers:

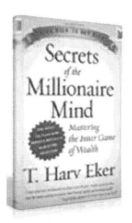

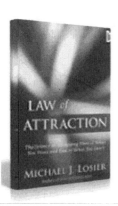

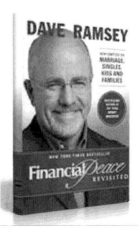

Chapter Three

The Empowered Prayer

"But without faith it is impossible to please him: for he that cometh to God must believe that he is, and that he is a rewarder of them that diligently seek him."

Hebrews 11:6

Power is truly given to men who pray. If you are going to make it today and have a healthy life, you have to pray. The "place" that I am in today with God spiritually was birthed out of a "floor" ministry. Everything I have and everything I do come from the time I spend with God. I don't need any more "lone ranger" endeavors and activities in my life that are not birthed out of the throne room of God. Since I have taken on this mindset, I have so much peace in my life that I am walking in increase constantly. I don't have enough time in the day to manifest all that God shares with me.

> *As I lay in God's presence, knowledge, ideas and creative solutions are dropped into my spirit by the Holy Spirit.*

Hidden Treasures of the Darkness

Proverbs 8:12, says that God will give us witty inventions. My entire life in Christ, I have had a strong prayer life. However, for the past 17 years, even more so the past 10 years, my prayer life has gone to new levels in the spirit. Much of this I know is contributed to the fact of my desire to obtain great wealth or acquire the riches of this world, so I can give liberally to kingdom projects. So as I lay in God's presence, knowledge, ideas and creative solutions are dropped into my spirit by the Holy Spirit. What I am experiencing in Christ now is a total different experience than in the past. The hidden treasures of the darkness are being revealed – *"And I will give thee the treasures of darkness, and hidden riches of secret places, that thou mayest know that I, the LORD, which call thee by thy name, am the God of Israel"* (Isaiah 45:3).

> *When you set yourself up to seek God, He will love you back.*

All of my technical and graphic design skills have mainly been taught to me by the Spirit of God. And if not taught, the Holy Spirit would direct me to a book and/or website where I could find the solution to the problem. The Holy Spirit has been such a teaching resource person in my life that I spend about 80% of time with God and 20% of my time with man. Meaning that, even while I am working in my office, I have soaking music on to foster a creative atmosphere so I can birth out newness at all times. There is a constant fluttering and stream of ideas activated in my office at all times.

Our entire Clark's Consultant Group was birthed out of this atmosphere as well. As I soaked in His presence, God visited me in a dream and showed me this business venture. When you set yourself up to seek God, He will love you back (Hebrews 11:6). I make a conscience effort every day to put myself under the presence of God that allows my spirit to be open to hear beyond the natural mind. David said, *"One thing have I desired of the LORD, that will I seek after; that I may dwell in the house of the LORD all the days of my life, to behold the beauty of the LORD, and to inquire in his temple"* (Psalm 27:4).

Notice in this scripture it says, dwell, and not stop by.

Dwell in the Hebrew means *to sit or remain.* These are never ending words for me. So we can create an environment that we can be with God at all times.

Soaking Prayers

One of the greatest moves that are sweeping across this nation now in the body of Christ is soaking prayers. It is learning how to be quiet in God's presence, so that He might impregnate us with His vision as well as empower us to do greater things for Him for His glory. Some have even been healed in His presence like this.

This is what has changed or sped up God moving in my life in such a powerful way. Things that in the past took years to happen, God is now doing it in a day or week or month.

As I soak in His presence, He downloads information, direction and technology to help me fulfill the mandate that is upon my life. I have never experienced anything like this before. It is amazing! All I can tell you; it works.

I don't have a copyright or patent on this, so everybody can take advantage of being in His presence like this. *It is a guarantee increase response.*

What is soaking?

Soaking is taking time to simply be quiet for moments in a day, silently laying before Him with soft soaking music playing, letting Him overshadow you.

No, soaking is not transcendental meditation or yoga. It's just laying in His presence – giving Him time to fellowship with you. We have to quiet our minds and spirits, so we can hear God more clearly. And soaking in His presence is an excellent way to do this.

Let's face it, this world is a noisy place, and until we can designate some respite times in our lives, we will never rest. Often we are like the proverbial rat or hamster running constantly on the wheel in a cave – never reaching a destination.

Soaking music

When you are intimate with your spouse, you don't put on loud or upbeat music; no, you play music that is conducive to the setting. This is what is required with times like this with the Father. There is so much wonderful soaking music out now. On the next page is a list of some of my favorite artists.

- Julie True
- Grace Williams
- Jason Upton
- Roberto & Kimberly Rivera
- Rick Pino

All of these artists' music is available on Youtube, Spotify, itunes and Pandora. The best way to enjoy these artists is to create a playlist. However, on Pandora, you cannot create a playlist, but you can set your radio station to one of these artists and it will find artists with similar sounds and play them. You want these sounds in your house all the time.

Here is a sample of a playlist a friend sent to me from Youtube. She put 49 videos on this playlist.

www.youtube.com

Below is a playlist I made of Grace Williams on Spotify. What I did was search for Grace Williams' name in the search finder and her music was found. Then I right clicked and created a Grace Williams playlist.

www.spotify.com

FYI: You would need to download the player onto your computer. Open up your internet browser and type in: www.spotify.com. When the pages open, select to download player.

Great Advice: Once you download Spotify player onto your computer, it will automatically open when you start up your computer. When this happens, it slows down your computer readiness for you to start working on it. To eliminate this, go into Preferences menu (Edit > Preferences on a Windows Machine, or Spotify > Preferences on a Mac), scroll to the bottom of that screen and click next to the *"Don't Open Automatically"* under the "System" tab.

Here's what Pandora's website looks like.

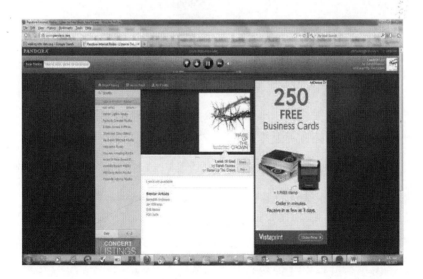

www.pandora.com

Another website you can visit and get some great soaking music from is Soaking.net: www.soaking.net. They already have a playlist of soaking music readily available for you to select and listen to. See a sample of the website on the next page.

www.soaking.net

Another player I take advantage of is Media Player. I can burn CD's on this player as well as create a playlist. Listen, I use every opportunity that I know that is available to me to create the world I want. And you need to do the same.

You cannot leave it up to chance when you are after your "gold." You have to have a strategic plan built around seeking God, His Word and faith to believe for the impossible.

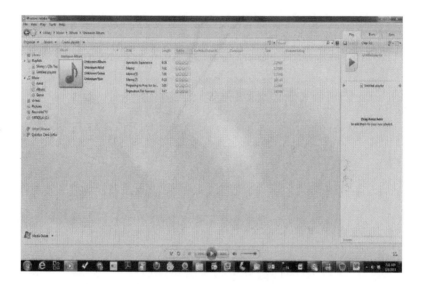

The bottom line: Soaking is more about you becoming one with Him, more acquainted with Him and understanding His ways, so that greater works can be done through you and in your life for the kingdom.

Acquiring God's Thoughts and Ways

Isaiah 55:8-9 says, *"For my thoughts are not your thoughts, nor are your ways my ways," says the* LORD. *"For as the heavens are higher than the earth, so are my ways higher than your ways, and my thoughts than your thoughts."*

Oh, how often we are quick to quote this scripture, that God's thoughts and ways are not our thoughts and ways as though we can never acquire God's thoughts and ways. But, I suggest to you that the gap between God's thoughts and ways and your thoughts and ways can be decreased if we would just lay out in His presence long enough to gain His insight.

> *God is able and wants to make His ways known unto us...We must want the GIVER more than GIFT.*

"He made known his ways unto Moses, his acts unto the children of Israel" (Psalm 103:7). God is able and wants to make His ways known unto us. He did it for Moses and He will do it for us. However, we must want the GIVER more than the GIFT.

Philippians 2:5 says, *"Let this mind be in you, which was also in Christ Jesus."* If we are to attain the mind of Christ, there is only one sure way to meet this goal – spending time with Him and in His Word.

We are the apple of God's eyes. We are *His* choice to fellowship with. *"For thus saith the LORD of hosts; After the glory hath he sent me unto the nations which spoiled you: for he that toucheth you toucheth the apple of his eye" (Zechariah 2:8). "Keep me as the apple of thy eye, hide me under the shadow of thy wings" (Psalm 17:8).*

God loves us and He wants to spend time with us. His eyes are forever upon His bride!

"The eyes of the LORD are upon the righteous, and his ears are open unto their cry." Psalm 34:15

"For the eyes of the Lord are over the righteous, and his ears are open unto their prayers: but the face of the Lord is against them that do evil." I Peter 3:12

"Behold, the eye of the LORD is upon them that fear him, upon them that hope in his mercy." Psalm 33:18

"For the eyes of the LORD run to and fro throughout the whole earth, to show himself strong in the behalf of them whose heart is perfect toward him. Herein thou hast

done foolishly: therefore from henceforth thou shalt have wars." 2 Chronicles 16:9

I don't know how much plainer I can say it. **God wants to spend time with His people.**

In the Old Testament there were three types of tabernacles that were built –The Tabernacle of Moses, The Tabernacle of David and Solomon's Temple. And the whole premise behind erecting these structures was that God's presence would have a place to dwell within. But now, in the New Testament, we are the temple of God. We are the dwelling place of God now – *"Know ye not that ye are the temple of God, and that the Spirit of God dwelleth in you?"* (I Corinthians 3:16)

If you want an empowered prayer life, spending time with God is not an option. It is a mandate! And it is out of this empowered life that God will open up the treasures of heaven to give us the hidden treasures of the darkness.

Wealth and honor are supposed to be in our house. Wealth and honor are the byproducts of Christians who seek God. Remember, Hebrews 6:12 tells us that God will reward those who diligently seek Him. A reward is something good and diligently means searching. In the

Hebrew the word *"reward"* means to deal bountifully with, wages, and gain.

God is not mad with us about increasing our holdings. In fact, He is the one that is going to give to us bountifully. As we seek Him, He releases blessings upon our lives that mirror our seeking. II Chronicles 26:5 says that as long as Uzziah sought the Lord, God prospered him.

God is not a deadbeat God. He wants His people to have everything that pertain to life and goodliness.

The word, sought, in the Hebrew means diligently inquire, research, investigate or consult. We have to have tenacity about seeking God. We must invite God into every affair of our lives. Everything that concerns us, God is concerned about. They that seek the Lord shall not want for any good thing according to the Psalmist, Psalm 34 and verses 8-10.

"O taste and see that the LORD is good: blessed is the man that trusteth in him. O fear the LORD, ye his saints: for there is no want to them that fear him. The young lions

do lack, and suffer hunger: but they that seek the LORD
shall not want any good thing."

The phrase, *"but they that seek the* LORD *shall not want
any good thing,"* in the Douay-Rheims Bible it says, *but
they that seek the Lord* **shall not be deprived of any
good.**

God is not a deadbeat God. He wants His people to have
everything that pertain to life and goodliness. You will
never see God's face on the side of a milk carton or
posted on a bulletin board in the post office. This is not
the God we serve. God has always taken care of His
people. 3 John, Chapter 1, verse 2 says, *"Beloved, I pray
that you may prosper in all things and be in health, just
as your soul prospers."*

If you are reading this book, your soul should be
prospering right now. Therefore, you are putting
yourself in a position more for God to bless you
financially. The words *"to prosper"* in this scripture
means to excel and succeed at something desirable, and
to advance to the highest place possible. There is
nothing wrong with being the best.

And also the word *"prosperity"* is synonymous with the
word *"success."* When we embrace this truth, we can

truly declare we are the head and not the tail. We are above and not beneath (Deuteronomy 28:13).

Now before, I leave this section; I want you to notice, the word *"wages"* also. Wages is a word associated with the job market. An employer pays wages to an employee for work **performed.** I wonder how much wages will some of you get if God had to pay you for the amount of time you spent seeking Him -- something to think about...huh.

For some, none! For others, a little! But for those of us who have been soaking in His presence and seeking Him relentlessly and intently, our rewards will be great.

Know Your Thoughts Afar Off

"Thou knowest my downsitting and mine uprising, thou understandest my thought afar off"

Psalms 139:2

Perhaps one of the most awesome things that has come out of me seeking God like this is that God is now fulfilling my thoughts. This started happening to me about three years ago (2010). I especially noticed it one day when I was driving down the highway on my way home from a meeting and I was thinking to myself how I might want to get involved in the Toastmasters Program. You see, I am always about sharpening and honing my skills. Immediately, I thought, I don't know anybody that is in this program to get some inside information now.

Soaking in God's presence has been one of the most rewarding and powerful things I have ever done in my life.

I was about 10 minutes from my home, and when I arrived home I went upstairs in my office to work. Within five minutes, my phone rang. It was a young lady I had not talked to in years; however, we were just reconnected through an event we were working on. As we were talking about the event, somehow it was brought up that she was involved in the Toastmasters Program. This literally "blew my mind." I did not ask her about this nor was it a part of our agenda. But God knew she had the answer to my need.

She shared with me everything I needed to get started – contact people, websites, the Toastmasters Program, locations, etc. When I say everything, I mean everything. She was knowledgeable of everything. This is what soaking in God's presence can lead to – God's fulfilling your thoughts.

Soaking in God's presence has been one of the most rewarding and powerful things I have ever done in my life.

Developing a Praying Spirit

Often when people encounter people of prayer like me, there is a misconception that we acquire this great desire and passion to pray through osmosis. But, we, like everyone else started our prayer life off just like you did. We had to learn how to pray. We had to learn what to pray. We had to learn when to pray, and then we had to pray.

There is only one **sure** way to developing a praying spirit and that is to PRAY!!! However, there is an art to praying. This was the only thing in scripture that the disciples asked Jesus to teach them. They said, Lord, teach us to pray.

The implication here is that the way they knew how to pray was incorrect because it was a custom of the Jewish community, of which they were, to go to the temple to pray at certain times and seasons. So them praying was not the issue, it was praying prayers that got results. So when they saw Jesus praying, and His prayers got results, they knew He knew something they did not know. Therefore, they asked Jesus to teach them how to pray.

He did and for three years they sat under His tutelage observing, listening and following Jesus' instructions in prayer, healing and evangelism. And after His death, they began their ministries with an established **SEASONED** prayer life.

When the disciples prayed in the book of Acts, often their prayers were cited for how powerful they were even to the point that a building shook one time because of their praying.

Prayer is only activated in our lives in a GREATER measure when we pray. The desire to pray gets stronger each time we activate prayer in our life. It is said that there are four primary reasons Jesus prayed:

1. Obedience - To obey the Father in all things
2. Unity - To become one with the Father
3. Model - To serve as a model for others to follow
4. Empowered - To become empowered to do the works of the kingdom

If we want to become extraordinary and do great works for the kingdom of God; then we must pray. We must develop a prayer life that not only strengthens our life, but also serves as a lifeline or catalyst for others to model.

Perhaps, you are reading this book and you are saying to yourself, all this sounds good and fine, but Dr. Clark you don't know my situation. I have tried many things to develop a strong prayer life, but nothing has really worked. I have a genuine desire to have a strong prayer life, but it seems as though I can never fulfill this desire in my life. I start out good, but over time, my prayer life dwindles down until it has floundered all together. If this is you, you are amongst the masses. Don't get discouraged just get up and try again. It is only a failure if you fail to try again.

In our Warrior's Bride School of Prayer, we have a course on *"How to Develop a Praying Spirit."* We know developing a praying spirit can be a difficult process for many in the body of Christ; so perhaps, these steps outlined on the next pages can assist you in developing a praying spirit.

A. Desire

The first step in developing a praying spirit is having the desire to pray. Believe it or not, but not everyone wants to develop a praying spirit. But if you are among the ones who have a heart panting for more of God, then I am talking to you. Basically, there are two elements to desire.

1. God: It is God's desire that we pray (Luke 18:1). God delights in our prayers (Proverbs 15:8).

2. Man: We must have a desire to pray. The development of a praying spirit always starts with a desire to pray as stated above (Proverbs 10:24, Psalm 37:4, 2 Corinthians 8:11-12).

   Desire means a strong conscious impulse to have, be or do something. We must be passionate about spending time with God.

B. Activate

The next step is to activate a prayer life with God.

1. Routine: Set up a prayer schedule (James 2:26, 5:16).

2. Pray: You have to pray to develop a praying spirit. Prayer is not something that you learn, but it is something that is learned through experience. *The only way you can fail in prayer is to fail to pray* (I Samuel 12:23).

C. Discipline

It is warfare to pray! Know that when you decide to spend more time with God in prayer, your flesh is going to fight against it. But you have to press in beyond your flesh.

1. Crucify: Put your body under subjection, when you are attempting to develop a praying spirit. You have to crucify the flesh (1 Corinthians 9:27,

Matthew 26:41, Galatians 2:20). You have to speak to your flesh and command it to come under subjection to the Spirit of God and the Word of God.

2. Sacrifice: Prayer has always been linked with a sacrifice. Prayer is not based on feelings (Genesis 22:1-13).

D. Prayer

When you are working on developing a praying spirit, don't forget to pray and invite the Holy Spirit to assist you in the process. Remember, He is our helper and guide.

1. Ask: Ask the Father to give you a praying spirit (I John 5:14-15, Matthew 7:7-8).

2. Confess: Confess that you have a praying spirit (Proverbs 18:21, Romans 4:17).

Increase Prophetic Insight

Jeremiah 33:3 says, *"Call unto me, and I will answer thee, and show thee great and mighty things, which thou knowest not."*

This verse in Jeremiah is a very powerful and prophetic scripture for those who pray. There is so much revelatory assurance in this scripture of what God wants to do for us if we would just call and cry out to Him.

First, it says, when we pray, He will answer us. Every time we pray in faith, we have God's full attention.

Second, when we get His attention, He will release prophetic insight for us to see and know things we have never known before.

People of God, THIS IS IT! We have to pull on this part "b" of this scripture like never before. We need insight in order for us to take the "land." It is the part "b" of this scripture where witty inventions and increase come from. God wants to show us great and mighty things.

Praying, soaking in His presence is where you will be enveloped and overshadowed by His presence like the Holy Spirit overshadowed Mary in Luke, Chapter 1, Verse 35. He will not only visit you, but He will ABIDE with you. You will hear things, you never heard before. You will see things, you have never seen before. This is a norm for God. He wants us to be impregnated with vision.

> *There is a progression with God that as we seek Him passionately, we will see new realms in the spirit and do things we have never done before.*

For the first time in my life I had an opened vision. God has already dealt with me in dreams, but I had never had a vision. About a month and a half before releasing this book, I had to speak in Tulsa, OK.

The day we arrived, we went straight to the church, and we were in service until late that afternoon. So when we checked into the hotel and I laid down in the bed to get some rest, before going back that night, as soon as I closed my eyes, I immediately had an open vision of our van being in a wreck. I saw our van running into another vehicle. It was a quick flash, and I knew it was a warning from God.

Immediately, I said to the other person in the room, we need to pray. I just saw us in a car accident. We immediately began to pray and come against it. That was Friday afternoon and that Saturday morning at the

1:00 p.m. service the host began sharing how they and the intercessors had been led to pray. They had been led to pray and war against car accidents that morning and the previous morning.

You see, God will show us things we know not. We were at a prayer conference where the leaders were strong people of prayer. And when you have developed a culture of prayer like they had in this ministry, everybody will pick up on the same thing. But what stood out the most in my spirit was that God was introducing to me another realm of prophetic insight – an open vision.

There is a progression with God that as we seek Him passionately, we will see new realms in the spirit and do things we have never done before. This is why I long to be with God more than with men. **I can do more with God than I can do with men!!!**

There is a prophetic insight that you will only get from seeking Him!!!

Chapter Four

The Empowered Entrepreneur

*"And you shall remember the LORD your God,
for it is He who gives you power to get wealth, that
He may establish His covenant which He swore to
your fathers, as it is this day."*

Deuteronomy 8:18

O ur motivation for accumulation should be distribution. In Genesis 12:2 it says, *"And I will make of thee a great nation, and I will bless thee, and make thy name great; **and thou shalt be a blessing.**"* And we see this confirmed again in I Timothy 6:17-19, *"Charge them that are rich in this world, that they be not highminded, nor trust in uncertain riches, but in the living God, who giveth us richly all things to enjoy; That they do good, that they be rich in good works, **ready to distribute,** willing to communicate; Laying up in store for themselves a good foundation against the time to come, that they may lay hold on eternal life* (King James Bible (Cambridge Ed.)

The solution to our problem is that the church not only be a spiritual entity in society, but an enterprising organism. We must raise up enterprising members...with a strong kingdom mandate to rule in the business gate.

When we acquire acquisition (gold, silver, houses, land, etc.), we are not to forget God. There is so much money that is needed in the kingdom of God in order for righteous causes to be financed. The solution to our problem is that the church not only be a spiritual entity in society, but an enterprising organism. We must raise up enterprising members within the house of the Lord with a strong kingdom mandate to rule in the business gate.

For far too long, the church has languished in this gate, if not totally abandoned it for the most part. When I teach on this in my travels globally, I share how the devil has "hoodwinked" us (the church) in this area. We have relegated our wealthy place to just collecting tithes & offerings and donations in the church. Because of this, the billions of dollars in corporate America are rarely in the hands of Christian people, while we still proclaim our Father owns the cattle on a thousand hills.

Hogwash….we are such an embarrassment to the kingdom of God.

If God is going to give us the hidden treasures in the darkness (Isaiah 45:3) or the riches of the wicked (Proverbs 13:22), then by now, the body of Christ overall should be walking in great wealth.

When God delivered the children of Israel out of the hand of Pharaoh, He gave them the wealth of the land.

"And I will give this people favor in the sight of the Egyptians: and it shall come to pass, that, when you go, you shall not go empty."

Exodus 3:21

The business gate or economic mountain, as stated in other publications, is an essential gate for the church to rule within. It is the business gate that is considered the centipede of any city. While the government gate is extremely important in a city as well, but it is the business gate that is the life-giving sustainability entity.

When a city is no longer flourishing and prospering financially, the city is doomed for ruin. Therefore, the business gate is the pivotal point for growth and development. It is also the gauge that is often looked at in determining your power and influence within a geographical area.

This is why the church must not only be considered a spiritual house, but an enterprising entity as well because whoever mans the business gate has a tremendous amount of power and influence.

I love what Ecclesiastes 9:16 says about this and because this is a powerful scripture that speaks volume to me, I am going to share several translations with you in hope that you get the point.

New International Version: So I said, "Wisdom is better than strength." But the poor man's wisdom is despised, *and his words are no longer heeded.*

New Living Translation: So even though wisdom is better than strength, those who are wise will be despised if they are poor. *What they say will not be appreciated for long.*

King James Bible: Then said I, Wisdom *is* better than strength: nevertheless the poor man's wisdom *is* despised, *and his words are not heard.*

New American Standard Bible: So I said, "Wisdom is better than strength." But the wisdom of the poor man is despised *and his words are not heeded.*

International Standard Version: So I concluded, "Wisdom is better than strength. Nevertheless, the wisdom of the poor is rejected—*his words are never heard.*"

NET Bible: So I concluded that wisdom is better than might, but a poor man's wisdom is despised; *no one ever listens to his advice.*

GOD'S WORD Translation: So I said, "Wisdom is better than strength," even though that poor person's wisdom was despised, *and no one listened to what he said.*

The main motif in this scripture is that if you are broke and poor, you have no voice. But the flip side of this is that if you are rich, you have a voice, an audience and influence.

> *If you are broke and poor, you have no voice.*

Here are some additional scriptures to affirm this as well:

"Seest thou a man diligent in his business? He shall stand before kings; He shall not stand before mean men." (Proverbs 22:29)

"The rich man's wealth is his strong city: the destruction of the poor is their poverty." (Proverbs 10:15)

The church has been without a "major" voice in the business sector far too long. Yes, we have always had a remnant, but according to the scriptures, the blessings of Abraham should be overtaking our lives because we are the seeds of Abraham -- **"And if ye be Christ's, then are ye Abraham's seed,** and heirs according to the promise"** (Galatians 3:29).

The question here should be, "What is the promise?"

We should be abundantly blessed – *"Now the LORD had said unto Abram, Get thee out of thy country, and from* *thy kindred, and from thy father's house, unto a land that I will shew thee: And I will make of thee a great nation, and I will bless thee, and make thy name great; and thou shalt be a blessing: And I will bless them that bless thee, and curse him that curseth thee: **and in thee shall all families of the earth be blessed"** (Genesis 12:1).*

Why does God want us to prosper? So we can be symbols of kingdom prosperity. When Isaac dwelt in the land of Gerar in Genesis 26:28, it says that when King Abimelech saw how Isaac was being blessed, he immediately credited it to that the Lord was with him.

The International Standard Version says: *"We've seen that the LORD is with you," they responded, "so we're proposing an agreement between us—between us and you. Allow us to make a treaty with you, by which you'll agree not to do us any harm, just as we haven't harmed you, since we've done nothing but good for you after we sent you away in peace. **As a result, you've been tremendously blessed by the LORD."***

The Era of Entrepreneurs

Everyone needs to be an entrepreneur!

In the 1996 book, "The Millionaire Next Door: The Surprising Secrets of America's Wealthy," the authors state that two-thirds of the millionaires are self-employed, with 75 percent of them entrepreneurs, and the remainder professionals such as doctors and accountants.

The more I interface with people who work in corporate America, the more and more this statement above is true. We have always had a generation of unhappy people working in corporate America (55%), but there was not much people could do about their situation many years ago. However, this is not true now. Mindsets and concepts have really changed about this.

Years ago, the traditional thinking and mindset about working in corporate America was that you go to school, get an education and then find a great job in a leading company. So the concept of going into business for yourself was almost unheard of. In fact, it was classified as being too risky and you probably would be just wasting your time.

But according to many economists, today, this is completely the opposite now. Today, it is more risky to work for corporate America. So today, it is far more *sensible* to be an entrepreneur.

Let's just face it; loyalty in corporate America has dramatically changed. But we have to be realists as well. Companies **only** hire you when there is a need for you. So when there is no need or not enough finances coming in to pay you for your service(s), then they have to let you go. **It just good business sense!**

> *Today, it is more risky to work for corporate America....it is far more sensible to be an entrepreneur*

Now, there are some loyalty issues and misappropriation of funds in some companies, but the simple business model is if you are needed, employers will hire you. If they don't need you or need you anymore; then employers will not hire you or they will lay you off. It is truly not personal, it is just business. So it is more risky to work for corporate America today, than to work for yourself.

Now, I am not telling you to quit your job. But what I am saying you need to even the playing field by knowing all of your options. Whatever knowledge you do **not** know, it is being used against you.

Home-based Business: One of the booming solutions to this problem is starting a home-based business. The tax write-offs alone should encourage everyone to start a home-based business. You can write off your internet service (start up and hosting fees); room usage, telephone, utilities (certain percentage), equipment, transaction banking fees, business luncheons and dinners, education materials, training, mileage, retirement options, health benefits, etc. These are all legitimate write-offs that the IRA gives to an entrepreneur. And, of course, you never just want to take a vacation anymore; you want to set your travels schedule around your business enterprises.

> *We have to stop trading our talent for time. Through entrepreneurship you can control which hours you want to work.*

It is said that one in every eight U.S. households contained a home-based business, and now 50% of all small firms are home-based businesses. People who stay at home and run their business from their home are touted *now* to have the edge.

What we have to do is stop trading our talent for time. Through entrepreneurship you can control *which* hours you want to work. I do this all the time. Now, this does not mean you will work less hours (more than likely you will work more hours, especially when you start), but at least you control *which* hours.

If I want to be free during the day, then I might set my work hours to be in the middle of the night or I might work until 12am or 12:30am. For me, I only need three to four hours of rest and I am good for an entire day. Sometimes I enjoy just sitting at home throughout the day watching DVDs. My work day would have been completed, so this afforded me the opportunity to relax – to have a better quality of life. I can take my mental health days when I want to. Plus, I can take my vacations when I want to. My entire business is mainly mobile, so I control everything electronically for the most part. Becoming an entrepreneur is a great way to integrate work into your home life.

Entrepreneurship is definitely the way to go, and it is growing tremendously and much of it is due to the technological age. In the '70s and '80s the big corporations were looked at as the best route to go or to assimilate within. They were looked at having the best of everything – technology, manufacturing and service.

But today, there is a growing consensus among consumers that bigger the company, the older and more out-of-date the technology. While this might not be exactly true, there is still an element of truth to consider.

When we received Christ into our lives, we are marked automatically for kingdom blessings.

We are a technological age, and in order for a company to be sustained in this generation, their technology must be geared toward a fast-moving, highly versatile business environment, with a synergy to meet not only our business needs, but our personal needs. It is said that it is the one-on-one transactions that are essential in this market, and the greatest opportunities are in entrepreneurship.

Marked For Blessings

When we received Christ into our lives, we are marked automatically for kingdom blessings. We are the blessed of the Lord and God's symbols to the world that He is good. The Bible says every good and perfect gift comes from the Father above (James 1:17). We are marked for greatness **and** increase.

From the beginning of time, we were marked for his greatness. This is how Zechariah 8:13 records it in the New Living Translation, *"Among the other nations, Judah and Israel became symbols of a cursed nation. But no longer!* ***Now I will rescue you and make you both a symbol and a source of blessing.*** *So don't be afraid. Be strong, and get on with rebuilding the Temple!*

And again in Psalm 67:5-7 of the Message Bible, *"God! Let people thank and enjoy you. Let all people thank and enjoy you. Earth, display your exuberance!* ***You mark us with blessing, O God, our God. You mark us with blessing,*** *O God. Earth's four corners - honor him!*

These are powerful scriptures. Let's settle this issue now, **YOU ARE MARKED FOR GREATNESS!** I like what Zig Ziglar says in his book, ***See You At The Top*** *-- "Man was designed for accomplishment, engineered for success and endowed with the seeds of greatness."*

God wants us so blessed that the world would marvel at us and our God. This is what happened with the Queen of Sheba in the book of I Kings, Chapter 10:1-10, when she saw how God had blessed Solomon.

"The queen of Sheba heard about Solomon and his connection with the Name of GOD. She came to put his reputation to the test by asking tough questions. She made a grand and showy entrance into Jerusalem— camels loaded with spices, a huge amount of gold, and precious gems. She came to Solomon and talked about all the things that she cared about, emptying her heart to him. Solomon answered everything she put to him— nothing stumped him. When the queen of Sheba experienced for herself Solomon's wisdom and saw with her own eyes the palace he had built, the meals that were served, the impressive array of court officials and sharply dressed waiters, the lavish crystal, and the elaborate worship extravagant with Whole-Burnt-Offerings at the steps leading up to The Temple of GOD, it took her breath away.

She said to the king, "It's all true! Your reputation for accomplishment and wisdom that reached all the way to my country is confirmed. I wouldn't have believed it if I hadn't seen it for myself; they didn't exaggerate! Such wisdom and elegance—far more than I could ever have imagined. Lucky the men and women who work for you, getting to be around you every day and hear your wise words firsthand! And blessed be GOD, your God, who took such a liking to you and made you king. Clearly, GOD's love for Israel is behind this, making you king to keep a just order and nurture a God-pleasing people.

She then gave the king four and a half tons of gold, and also sack after sack of spices and expensive gems. There hasn't been a cargo of spices like that since that shipload the queen of Sheba brought to King Solomon" (Message Bible).

This is an excellent example of what God has created us to be – *A Symbol of His Blessings!*

And in the book of Zechariah, Chapter 9 verses 16-17, this is stated as well.

*As long as we are broke, busted and disgusted, we are **not** a good symbol for God.*

"And the LORD their God shall save them in that day as the flock of his people**: for they shall be as the stones of a crown, lifted up as an ensign upon his land.** For how great is his goodness, and how great is his beauty! corn shall make the young men cheerful, and new wine the maids."

The phrase "lifted up as an ensign" in the Hebrew means to gleam from afar, to be conspicuous as a signal, a flag fluttering in the wind, a sign, a banner, an emblem. God wants the people of the world to see all the good that He does for His people, so that they might be drawn to Him (see Jeremiah 33:9 NLT).

You see, as long as we are broke, busted and disgusted, we are **not** a good symbol for God. And I might go so far to say, we are an embarrassment to Him. When you are poor, you have no "voice." No one wants to listen to poor people, so I agree with the book of Ecclesiastes, *"Wisdom is better than strength. Nevertheless, the wisdom of the poor is rejected—**his words are never heard.**"*

Seat At The Table Or On The Menu

As I delve into this segment, I want to give credit where credit is due. So I want to credit this segment of teaching to one of our regional Apostles in North Carolina, Apostle Calvin Ellison. I heard this teaching from him first, and it made an indelible mark upon my heart and spirit.

Apostle Ellison is a marketplace leader in his region and he sits on several city and state boards, which allows him to interface with over 300 organizations and non-profit agencies. He said in his years of working with these organizations, he found that many church leaders always wanted a hand out instead of a hand up. In other words, they always wanted to be on the menu and not have a seat at the table.

The menu is symbolic of you looking to others to meet your needs or give you what you want versus having a seat at the table to be a part of the decision-making body to direct the funds. As well, being on the menu is symbolic of being poor versus being seated at the table, which is symbolic of being rich.

So let's look at this scripture again -- *"Wisdom is better than strength. Nevertheless, the wisdom of the poor is rejected—**his words are never heard.**"*

When we want to be on the menu more than we want to be seated at the table, then we will never have the impact that the Lord is desiring that we have in our communities, cities and states.

When we (the church) are on the menu instead of being seated at the table, we will always relegate and relinquish our opportunity to use our impact and influence for the kingdom of God. We should be in control not subservient to or at the mercy of those that do not know our God. So when we want to be on the menu more than we want to be seated at the table, then we will never have the impact that the Lord desires that we have in our communities, cities and states.

City transformation and reformation will only take place when we are in place. And too many of us are out of place. The Greek definition for church is *"Ekklesia."* It is the definition for rulership. In church history, the church was the political seat for decision-making for cities. It was the lawgivers and lawkeepers in communities. It was also responsible for electing city officials, assisting in city planning, creating policies as well as governing the city overall. In every arena, righteous people were expected to lead. They were the judges, the kings and Prime Ministers.

But somewhere along the line, we lost our seat **and** our voice. However, right now, we are striving to get both of these back. The devil has hoodwinked us long enough. I thank God today that more and more pastors and leaders in the body of Christ have embraced this revelation and truth and setting up Business Incubation Centers in their churches as well as participating in the city government. This is an incredible feat and vision in the universal church as a whole. What pastors now are attempting to do is to identify and empower people to seek out entrepreneurship. With ongoing training and a support system in place to encourage the neophyte entrepreneur, the desired end result then is an empowered entrepreneur.

Definitely, the church is moving in the right direction, and I would encourage these pastors that have embraced marketplace ministry to continue on this path. This is the will of God and because it is the will of God, it will bear fruit if you don't faint in the day(s) of adversity. *"But he shall receive a hundredfold now in this time, houses, and brothers, and sisters, and mothers, and children, and lands, with persecutions; and in the world to come eternal life" (Mark 10:30).*

We Lack Nothing

When God delivered the children of Israel from under the hand of the Pharaoh, He made sure that they would lack nothing as I stated earlier – *"And I will give this people favor in the sight of the Egyptians: and it shall come to pass, that, when you go, you shall not go empty" (Exodus 3:21).* We have to know that we know that God is not the God of lack. He is the God of abundance! *"And all these blessings shall come on thee, and overtake thee, if thou shalt hearken unto the voice of the Lord thy God"* (Deuteronomy 28:2).

I have been poor and I have been rich and rich is better.

In the Brenton Translation of this scripture it says that the blessings shall find you. Do you know if you are walking in obedience to God's Word and seeking Him more than you are seeking things that blessings are trying to find you? Wow...this is awesome!

> *Lack is not of God...The Lord is our shepherd and we shall not want (Psalm 23:1).*

Listen, God is able to make all grace abound toward us. Whatever we need, the Apostle Paul tells us in 2 Corinthians 9:8 that we have all sufficiency. The Revised Standard Version says that you may **always** have enough of everything. When we embrace this truth, we can truly say with the Psalmist, no good thing will He withhold from those who walk uprightly (Psalm 84:11).

When God was talking to the Prophet Jeremiah in the 23rd chapter about the shepherds He was going to raise up, one of the things that He promised was that there would be no lack among them. *"And I will set up* *shepherds over them which shall feed them: and they shall fear no more, nor be dismayed, **neither shall they be lacking.***"

Lack is not of God. You are never going to convince me that lack is of God. I grew up in lack and you can't tell me that God was happy that I was made fun of in school because I lacked the proper clothes to wear.

The Lord is my Shepherd, and I shall not want (Psalm 23:1). You have to prophecy this scripture to yourself, to your mind, to your pocketbook, to your bank account; basically to everything....**YOU SHALL NOT WANT!**

YOU HAVE TO SAY IT UNTIL IT MANIFEST IN YOUR LIFE!!!!

God is your source. Whatever it takes to ingrain this into your mind and spirit, you got to do it. Because the negative forces that are in this world are forever pulling on us to believe different. This is why you have to occasionally act like a crazy person and let the devil know, **you will not be moved.**

Money Cometh to Me Now

Years ago, I heard the pastor who coined this statement, "Money cometh to me now," at a service at my church. While it sounded cute and catchy, I really didn't fancy it. It just seemed too clichés to me, and frankly I thought it was just another ploy for the body of Christ to get hyped up on. You know we are good for this. But regardless, I really wasn't for it or against it, so I never repeated it.

You know in the body of Christ, we have a lot of sayings and I am not one to just jump into saying everything I hear preachers say. One thing I have learned during my walk in Christ is that we all have different experiences in Him and because of this; we often get revelation about things that is relevant actually ONLY for our personal situation. I know this and I am very watchful about this. So when new revelation is shared about something like this from the pulpit, I don't readily embrace it. Such as with this statement when the pastor had us repeating it after him. While I repeated it from an obedience standpoint, I still did not have the full revelation of this request. It just did not make **sense** to me.

Well, about ten years later, as I was studying on finance in the Bible, I ran over some information that "sealed the deal" in my heart about this statement. In one of the financial manuals I was working through, they quoted Hebrews, Chapter 10 and verse 35, *"Cast not away therefore your confidence, which has great recompense of reward."*

I found out that *"recompense of reward"* in the Greek was Mistha-Podosia. Mistha meant pay, salary, money, and payment of wages due. And Podosia meant feet or one in this field traveling on feet. I could not believe what I had just read. *"Money cometh to me now,"* does have a biblical origin.

> *Now that we know that God wants us blessed and wealthy. We have to fight like we never fought before.*

Needless to say, I began quoting this immediately. If I can find it in the Bible, then it belongs to me. I even put the declaration up on my office door that was in this manual. I am determined to get my daddy's (Father God) stuff back from the devil. We have got to get the money back into the hands of the people in the body of Christ that knows what money is for – to fund the gospel.

Here is the declaration that was in this manual:

MONEY, I SUMMON YOU

I HEREBY CALL YOU TO APPEAR

YOU HAVE FEET AND YOU ARE

COMING MY WAY

I AM A MONEY MAGNET

MONEY COMETH TO ME, NOW

IN JESUS NAME

Marketplace Intercessors

Now that we know that God wants us blessed and wealthy. We have to fight like we never fought before. This battle is like no others; it is the battle for the business gate. Because the devil knows what a powerful force the church will become as well as their members if we ever control this gate. Recognizing that we are engaging in a different type of warfare now, the church is now raising up marketplace intercessors. These intercessors have their hearts in the throne room of God and have their eyes and ears in the marketplace. These are also intercessors that know how to war correctly regarding marketplace ministry and how to release the greatness of God upon a church, individual and a business.

Marketplace intercessors are trained intercessors, which are trained in high level intercession to flow prophetically with a marketplace anointing. They also understand marketplace concepts; therefore, they seek constantly ways to stir up the entrepreneur spirit within their lives and in the lives of others. They are stalwarts in the realm of the spirit in releasing increase.

How do I know it? Because for an entire year, God had me to employ a marketplace intercessor for my business. When God challenged me about doing this, initially, I was not going to do it at least not at that moment. You see, when God spoke this to my spirit

> *Marketplace intercessors are trained intercessors, which are trained in high level intercession to flow prophetically with a marketplace anointing.*

to hire a marketplace intercessor for my business, my husband and I had a certain amount of income coming into our household. But for some reason, as soon as God instructed me to do this, we had a decrease in our household income. So I rationalized it and said well, maybe it's not for now. When our income increases again, I will start then.

The Sunday following this week, when all of this happened, I was sitting up in the balcony of my church. All of sudden, God interrupted my life, and shouted in my spirit, "If you are going to wait for every circumstance to be right before you obey ME, then you will never receive all that I have for you. I said hire your intercessor now." I couldn't wait for church service to end. I found the intercessor that God wanted me to hire in the lobby, handed her the check, and wrote on the check memo section, *"Pray without ceasing."* I told her I was hiring her to be a marketplace intercessor for our business. The exact amount I gave her was the exact amount she needed to take care of a financial need in her life that week.

People of God, we got to obey God! When I obeyed God, that following Monday, doors began to open for me immediately. I remember having so many networking opportunities availed to me. It was like the floodgates had opened. But that was not the main reason God was instructing me to do this. The main reason, which I found out later, was that He was preparing me for my next level of elevation.

The following year, God directed me to raise up marketplace intercessors. While I was aware of what God was doing with intercessors in the marketplace, not once did I think God was going to birth a marketplace leadership institute through me. In fact, when He spoke it to my spirit in my car on my way home from a marketplace training, I was like, "Oh, Lord, no! I am too busy for this."

We are anointed by God to do business on behalf of the King.

Now, I've been saved long enough to know I can't out talk God. As He impressed it upon my spirit more and more heading home, I finally said okay, but I also said I have to have a director. I am not doing this without a director. By noon the following day, God had appointed a former director of a Vocational School, which was licensed by the state of Texas to call me. I had not seen this woman for years. In the previous year, I did speak to her via phone at least one time, but that was it. But all of a sudden, "out of the blue," she called me. About ten minutes into the call, I realized what her call was all about. Once my spirit was enlightened to why she was calling me, I let her know why she was calling, and what I had asked God for. So I shared the vision with her and she was ecstatic. She immediately accepted the position as the Director of the Institute, and in four days, God had supplied instructors, staff, advisory board members, and a website was designed. All God wants us to say is yes to His will and He will fill in the blank.

We are heading into our fourth year of training and raising up marketplace intercessors and I love it. I love teaching and training God's people how to get their daddy's stuff – *"The earth is the LORD's, and the fullness thereof; the world, and they that dwell therein."* There is no need in us being without when God has given us **all** things that pertaineth to life and godliness.

The name of our Institute is **Anointed For Business Leadership Institute.** We are anointed by God to do business on behalf of the King. We accept this calling and we are excited about what the Lord wants to do through us. We have three programs now: Marketplace Intercessors, Business Entrepreneurs and our Warrior's Bride School of Prayer. This year we will be adding our Leadership Module. We are not completely sure where all God is going to take us, but the most important thing is that we are open and available to His leading.

Sow Your Way Out, Sow Your Way In

When I was working in corporate America, I never made over $23,000 a year. Needless to say, I was broke, and I could barely pay my bills. The house I was renting cost $230 a month and it was a challenge to put this "large" amount out (back then it looked like $2000) for one bill. But my sister and I had moved into this house initially together, so it wasn't so bad. It was only after she got married that this became a strain on me to pay every month along with the other utilities and household needs. So eventually, I had to consider working a second job. I did not have to look far to get a second job because one of the ladies that worked with me told me about a job after hours whereby I could help clean up office buildings. Well, it turned out to be the building I was working at during the day. So I was working at this building during the day and cleaning it up during the night.

As I was working both jobs, it never felt good to me. Somehow I knew this was not God's will or best for me. So as I was reading and meditating on the Word one day, I ran over the scripture in 2 Corinthians 9:10 whereby it said God will give seed to the sower. Immediately, when I read it, I knew this was my breakthrough scripture.

When I began to pray this scripture over my life, I heard in my spirit that someone was going to give me $100. So every day after work as soon as I would walk into my house, I would head straight to my bedroom, open my Bible to this verse, bow down and start praying over this scripture and releasing it over my life.

This went on for two weeks, and on one Wednesday around 11 p.m., as I was pulling up in front of my house from working my second job; a friend of mine had just pulled up in his car. This friend stayed on the next street over, so he decided to stop by to drop something off to me that someone had given to him for me that night at church. Before he could hand it to me, I told him, I know what it is. He was holding in his hand a white envelope. I told him to open it up and inside of it will be $100. He opened it and inside of it was a check for $100. I told him what I was believing God for and that was the answer to my prayer.

I couldn't wait to get to church on the following Sunday morning to put that $100 in the offering. I knew what God had given was a seed to break the poverty cycle and spirit of lack off of my life. This seed did so much for me that I cannot tell you when I quit that second job. All I know, I never had to work another second job in my life. In fact, what I made in a year, God has multiplied this over and over again.

But today, I am still sowing into the kingdom of God. In fact, I just realized that Shirley Clark Ministries sowed into kingdom endeavors about 30% of all the income that came into the different streams under the umbrella of Shirley Clark International Ministries. I had no idea until my husband and I were recording my giving for 2012. It was then I realized how much I had sowed into the work of the kingdom. This really blessed me when I realized how much I had sowed into the kingdom of God.

> *When there is a need, you need to plant a seed.*

We have to continually sow our way into situations and sow our way out of situations. This is a never ending cycle. If you want the blessings of God to continue to flow into your life, you have to be a sower. And you have to sow in season and out of season. Meaning, you can't wait for everything to be right before you start sowing. When there is a need, you need to plant a seed.

A farmer knows if he or she does not plant seeds there will be no harvest. Ecclesiastes 11:4 says, (New Living Translation) *"Farmers who wait for perfect weather never plant. If they watch every cloud, they never harvest."* The King James Version say, *"He that observeth the wind shall not sow; and he that regardeth the clouds shall not reap."*

So why do you think you are going to get a harvest when you have not planted seeds. It does not work this way. If God has blessed you financially, then you are obligated to sow even the more. No, I can't tell you scientifically how this works, but all I know is that it does work. Proverbs 11:24-25 says, *"There is that scattereth, and yet increaseth; and there is that withholdeth more than is meet, but it tendeth to poverty. The **liberal** soul shall be made fat: and he that watereth shall be watered also himself.*

When there is need, plant a seed!

Give Your Seed An Assignment

When a farmer plants corn seeds, he expects a corn harvest. When a farmer plants tomato seeds, he expects a tomato harvest. When a farmer plants cucumber seeds, he expects a cucumber harvest. So the seeds he plants have an assignment.

As it is with the natural, it is with the spirit. Since money is fluid – currency – we have to tell our money, when we sow, its target objective. I never really thought much about this until I heard a minister at a friend's church teach on this. He had a great anointing in the financial realm, so he had my attention -- and even more so now since I learned that when he started his business, he made 300 million dollars in five years. I knew this was somebody I need to listen and avail myself to.

From the time I heard him teach this about five years ago until now (2013), every time I sow a seed, I give it an assignment. I cannot tell you how much this teaching has enriched my life. I tried it and it works. I have increase in all areas of my life. Right now, things are coming to fruition quicker than I have ever seen in the past. It is overwhelming me! Every seed I sow has an assignment now. So every time you sow from this point on, you need to write on the back of the envelope or somewhere on it, what you want that seed to produce or harvest.

Wisdom of Solomon

As I was beginning to activate and learn more about the principle of naming your seed, God also taught me not to just focus on asking Him for things, but to also recognize how important it was for me to ask Him for the wisdom of Solomon and for favor. When God asked Solomon what He wanted from Him; and out of all the things Solomon could have asked for, but he only asked for wisdom to judge God's people. And because this was all he asked for, God gave him the riches of the land. *"And God said to Solomon, Because this was in thine heart, and thou hast not asked riches, wealth, or honour, nor the life of thine enemies, neither yet hast asked long life; but hast asked wisdom and knowledge for thyself, that thou mayest judge my people, over whom I have made thee king: Wisdom and knowledge is granted unto thee; and I will give thee riches, and wealth, and honour, such as none of the kings have had that have been before thee, neither shall there any after thee have the like"* (2 Chronicle 1:11-12).

In this season in my life, whatever I heard God tell me to do, I did it.

God began to impress in my spirit how favor will open up and cause a lot of the things that I was believing Him for to come to pass. While it was fine to name my seed, He said, but make sure that seed(s) will also produce wisdom, counsel, guidance, direction and favor in and on my life.

He said as I move you up or elevate you, I would have to have a great deal of wisdom to operate at the level He was going to take me. He wanted me to really hone in on these attributes.

In this season in my life, whatever I heard God tell me to do, I did it. I did not ask for anybody else's approval or assessment, I just did it. I have so much favor in my life right now that at times when I think about it, I almost want to cry.

The calls and emails that come into my home and office that confirm this favor is beyond reasoning. God really does want to favor Zion (you, His church, His body) in this season.

Increase is available for those who *diligently* seek Him.

What are my future financial aspirations?

1. Give 90% of my income to kingdom endeavors and live off 10%
2. Pay my tithes one year in advance

According to Pastor George Pearsons and Gloria Copeland in their *50 Days of Prosperity* teaching manual, there are 21 ways God supplies our needs and there are 191 scriptures associated with these ways. This was such a great list that I wanted to share it with you. However, I am not going to list all the scriptures he noted, so here is an abridged compilation of the text. Here is the list.

- Tithing: Malachi 3:10

- Sowing and Reaping: Genesis 8:22

- The Law of Multiplication: Mark 4:20

- Giving to the Poor: Matthew 19:21

- The Ministry: 2 Chronicles 20:20 *GOOD SUCCESS*

- Memorial Giving: Acts 10:4 *my prayers & charities have not gone unnoticed by God*

- Our Relationship With God: Matthew 6:33-34

- Provision Direct From the Throne: Hebrews 4:16

- By Creation, Re-creation and Restoration: John 6:11

- Miraculous Provision: Deuteronomy 15:1-2

- Earth's Resources: Psalm 67:5-6

- Hidden Treasures of Darkness: Isaiah 45:3

- Provision by Individuals: Luke 6:38

- God Uses Us: Proverbs 10:14 *wise men stored up knowledge But the mouth of a fool invites ruin.*

- Witty Inventions: Proverbs 8:12

- Simply the World's System: Ecclesiastes 2:26

- Angels: Psalm 103:20-21

- Wildlife: I Kings 17:4-6

- Because the Lord Needs It: Mark 14:13-16

- Our Covenant Inheritance: Hebrews 6:12

- The Favor of God: Exodus 11:3

God knows what His people need and He knows how to bless His people.

> *The Word works when we operate in it correctly. We can't do our own thing and expect to get the blessing or blessings that are laid up for those who walk up rightly before Him.*

"If ye then, being evil, know how to give good gifts unto your children: how much more shall your heavenly Father give the Holy Spirit to them that ask him?" (Luke 11:13)

"Every good gift and every perfect gift is from above, and comes down from the Father of lights, with whom is no variableness, neither shadow of turning." (James 1:17)

Seek the Kingdom First

If you have been saved for over five years or more, I know this might sound like a broken record. But it stands to be repeated because of the **impact** it will make in your life from a longevity standpoint if you keep your focus as God begins to bless you.

We are never to chase or seek blessings, we are to seek God. Matthew 6:33 says we are to seek the kingdom of God and His righteousness, and all these other "things" will be added to us.

Most of everything we want in this earth is "things." I have good news, God is not mad with us having things. We just have to seek Him and want Him **more** than the "things." I am convinced if we will seek God **and** His righteousness, He truly will supply all of our needs. **AGAIN, HE IS NOT A DEADBEAT DAD!**

"As long as I sought the LORD, and he heard me, and delivered me from all my fears"

Proverbs 8:17-21 in the Living Bible says, *"I love all who love me. Those who search for me shall surely find me. Unending riches, honor, justice and righteousness are mine to distribute. My gifts are better than the purest gold or sterling silver! My paths are those of justice and right. **Those who love and follow me are indeed wealthy: I fill their treasuries.**"*

Our hearts have to be right and tenderized if we are going to walk in the blessings of God. It is about seeking Him and His kingdom that He is now pouring out His blessings upon His people. In fact, it has never been about anything else, but this. Paul says in Philippians, that I might know Him in the power of His resurrection and fellowship of His suffering.

God will give you all you have need of from the wealth of His glory; we just have to seek the kingdom first. So often we put other things before Him and expect a favorable outcome. It won't work. It's called proper alignment. The Word works when we operate in it correctly. We can't do our own thing and expect to get the blessing or blessings that are laid up for those who walk up rightly before Him.

Seek first, not second, not third, but first.

Who do you call on when you get in trouble? Do you cry out to God first? Or do you call the doctor first? God is not mad that you go to the doctor; He just wants to be considered first. The sooner we put Him into the equation, the sooner we can get a breakthrough. *"And Asa in the thirty and ninth year of his reign was diseased in his feet, until his disease became severe: yet in his disease he sought not to the LORD, but to the physicians"* (2 Chronicles 16:12). Another translation says, *instead of asking the LORD for help, he went to doctors.* When you leave God out of the equation or seek Him last, you set yourself up for additional anguish and pain.

In the book of Jeremiah, Chapter 10 and verse 21, some of the pastors in his era were guilty of this. They were doing things their way and not seeking God. So God had the Prophet Jeremiah to address this. He said, *"For the pastors are become brutish, and have not sought the LORD: therefore they shall not prosper, and all their flocks shall be scattered."* In the Holman Christian Standard Bible, it says it this way, *"For the shepherds are stupid: they don't seek the LORD. Therefore they have not prospered, and their whole flock is scattered."*

> *The issue is not about serving God, but seeking God. We have a lot of servants, but not a lot of seekers.*

Pastors, if people are leaving your church constantly and it seem as though you cannot get a breakthrough in your finances; perhaps, this might be the reason. Perhaps, you are doing things your way and not God's way. In the Old Testament, in 2 Chronicles, Chapter 26 and verse 5, it says long as King Uzziah sought God, he prospered.

Servants Versus Seekers

You see the issue is not about serving God, but seeking God. We have a lot of servants, but not a lot of seekers.

We are supposed to be prosperous. In order for this to happen, though, we have to get beyond the Martha spirit (serving spirit) and cultivate the Mary spirit (worshipping spirit) more. Both spirits are necessary in the house of the Lord, but we often lack or neglect the one that empowers us to serve. We have to seek God in all of our dealings.

Remember, He can do exceedingly abundantly above....

It's about Him and not us!!!!

God Wants You to Be a Millionaire

For the past four or five years, most of the books I have read and study from were books written by millionaires. I believe strongly in my heart that I will be a millionaire. Over the years, I have had ministers prophesy this to me, but I have always felt in my heart this is one of the destinies God has for me. So for the past four or five years, most of my mentors and teachers have been millionaires. I believe if I am going to be a millionaire, then I needed to know how millionaires think.

I would go to the library and check out three or four books at a time written by millionaires. I would devour these books. Pulling out of them quotes, techniques and principles that they have used on their way to becoming a millionaire and what they are doing to maintain this lifestyle.

Over the years, I have learned a lot.

Then God brought people into my life who was millionaires. So I was able to glean up close and personal from people of this caliber. My life has truly been enriched by these encounters. I will be forever grateful to God for this. I feel I am a better person today than I was ten years ago because of these people.

My mindset, thoughts and actions are totally different. The way I process things now are completely opposite from the way I use to process things. IT'S A WHOLE NEW WORLD FOR ME! It does matter who you sit under and associate with. So much increase has come on and in my life that it is phenomena.

I know this stuff works what I am talking about in this book. I am a living testimony. But what I am most concerned about or aware of might be a better way to say it is that I do it right and that I keep the right attitude and mindset in the midst of being blessed. This is why I am very passionate about us seeking God.

> *Money is never evil. Rather it is the person that has the money that determines whether the money will be used for evil or good.*

You see, I had a personal friend that I saw God bless financially tremendously and I saw him lose it all to the point he could barely get a Wal-Mart job. So it is not just about the getting, it is about the keeping as well. And the best way to maintain your wealthy place is to remember the Lord for He truly is the One that gives us power to get wealth (Deuteronomy 8:18).

When God opened the door for this person to make a quarter of a million dollars in a year, he lost his value. He started partying and doing things that did not please God. If you have character issues now, then when you get money it is only going to escalate – become more visible. So you want to start working on your character and relationship with God now, so this won't be a stumbling block to you when God gives you money.

Money is never evil. Rather it is the person that has the money that determines whether the money will be used for evil or good. The love of money is the root of all evil (I Timothy 6:10).

God wants us to have good success.

Joshua 1:8 says, *"This book of the law shall not depart out of thy mouth; but thou shalt meditate therein day and night, that thou mayest observe to do according to all that is written therein: for then thou shalt make thy way prosperous, and then thou shalt have good success."*

> *Good success is guaranteed to those who continually walk after righteousness not greed.*

The New Living Translation says, *"Study this Book of Instruction continually. Meditate on it day and night so you will be **sure** to obey everything written in it. **Only** then will you prosper and succeed in all you do.*

Good success is guaranteed to those who continually walk after righteousness, not greed. We have to remember God not just in our season of lack, but in our season of abundance as well. *"For they got **not** the land in possession by their own sword, neither did their own* arm save them: but your right hand, and your arm, and the light of your countenance, because you had favor unto them" (Psalm 44:3).

There was a man in one of my classes when I was teaching on Faith and Finances at my church, who had a very sad story about money, God, and his life. He shared with the class that he grew up in a family where his parents were missionaries. They were the old school thinking missionaries. The poorer you are, the holier you are. Because of this, they were the "real" missionaries who were doing the work of the kingdom.

He said the day came when as a child he saw his daddy going through a garbage can looking for food. This made an indelible bad impression on his heart about God. So when he grew up, he turned his back on God. He wanted nothing to do with God. He said what kind of a God would have people eating out of a garbage can. So his mission in life – make as much money as he could and he did make a lot of money.

In his lifetime, he succeeded to the point where he was making 25 million dollars a year. He said he was determined to never be broke another day in his life. But the only problem with his plan was that when he got the money, he was not happy. His plan was flawed. He lost everything he valued and loved – his wife and children.

He worked so much that he never spent the time with them to cultivate a relationship.

So now, divorced and his relationship strained with his children, he is now seeking God for direction in his life and for God to help him with his relationship with his children. He was excited to tell us that he had joined the church the previous year and had tithed for the first time in his life. He had come to grips that the way his parents portrayed God in his life was incorrect and that God was not the reason they lived the way they lived. It was the lack of understanding of the Word of God and interpreting it incorrectly. The little boy inside of him finally grew up, and he was able to make peace with his past.

You see, in the body of Christ we must strengthen our relationship with and about money. We can have wrong examples and teachings in our lives about money. And whatever we saw and/or were taught as we were growing up is the attitude and behavior we most likely will adopt. God wants us to have money, but He wants us to have good success with the money. *"The blessing of the Lord, it makes rich, **and he adds no sorrow with it"*** (Proverbs 10:22).

Making Room For the New

As I stated earlier, I have spent the last four to five years reading books written by millionaires. I remember reading in one of the books that "you" desiring to be a millionaire does not take anything from anyone else in this world. It said sometimes people are concerned about this. Well, if I made this much money, I must be hindering someone else from having this or that. This book debunked this mindset. It said that there are 28 trillion dollars in the world economy and you getting a million do not hinder anybody else from getting what they want in life. Basically, this thinking is a trick of the devil. It is one of the lies that the devil tells us to keep us from prospering.

The devil knows if the body of Christ overall controls the business gate or mountain as a whole, the kingdom of God will be expanded in a greater measure. The church would have such an impact and influence that it would be debilitating to his kingdom and his vices. Jesus was manifested that He might destroy the works of the devil. And when He died on the cross, He handed this authority to us (Matthew 28:18). Now, we are the Ambassadors of Christ: we are the enforcers of the Kingdom of God's policies in this earth.

The challenge that is put before us now is taking our rightful place back in society. That is to own, dominate, influence and control. The only way to do this is through position and power. We must be positioned properly in the business community, be a business owner or entrepreneur and we must have power, heading up businesses and boards.

This model is not new to God. He gave us acquisition and dominion at the very beginning of time – *"And God said, Let us make man in our image, after our likeness: and let them have dominion over the fish of the sea, and over the fowl of the air, and over the cattle, and over all the earth, and over every creeping thing that creepeth upon the earth"* (Genesis 1:26).

> *The devil knows if the body of Christ overall controls the business gate or mountain as a whole, the kingdom of God will be expanded in a greater measure.*

And let them have dominion – See, we can stop right here.

In other translations it says: *They will rule…Let them be master.*

In Barnes' Notes this is recorded about this statement:

*"The relation of man to the creature is now stated. It is that of sovereignty. Those capacities of right thinking, right willing, and right acting, or of knowledge, holiness, and righteousness, in which man resembles God, qualify him for dominion, and constitute him lord of all creatures that are destitute of intellectual and moral endowments. Hence, wherever man enters he makes his sway to be felt. He contemplates the objects around him, marks their qualities and relations, conceives and resolves upon the end to be attained, and endeavors to make all things within his reach work together for its accomplishment. This is to rule on a limited scale. The field of his dominion is "the fish of the sea, the fowl of the skies, the cattle, the whole land, and everything that creepeth on the land." The order here is from the lowest to the highest…The primeval and prominent objects of human sway are here brought forward after the manner of Scripture. **But there is not an object within the ken of man which he does not aim at making subservient to his purposes.** He has made the sea his highway to the ends of the earth, the stars his pilots on the pathless ocean, the sun his bleacher*

and painter, the bowels of the earth the treasury from which he draws his precious and useful metals and much of his fuel, the steam his motive power, and the lightning his messenger. These are proofs of the evergrowing sway of man."

In Clark's Commentary of the Bible this is stated:

"Hence we see that the dominion was not the image. God created man capable of governing the world, and when fitted for the office, he fixed him in it. We see God's tender care and parental solicitude for the comfort and well-being of this masterpiece of his workmanship, in creating the world previously to the creation of man. *He prepared every thing for his subsistence, convenience, and pleasure, before he brought him into being; so that, comparing*

When we view things from this "higher" level thinking or perception, we will see the world around us differently. The way we do business, the way we manage our lives, and the way we talk will model this thinking.

little with great things, the house was built, furnished, and amply stored, by the time the destined tenant was ready to occupy it."

The whole premise behind this statement is that man was in charge. Our current reality is not our total reality. Our reality must be gauged from the Truth of God's Word and the sum total of our history and current existence. Our perception and understanding of who we are is always flawed and warped if we look only through the lenses and filters of our human existence. We must look at our eternal pedigree to perceive or comprehend our existence status.

When we view things from this "higher" level thinking or perception, we will see the world around us differently. The way we do business, the way we manage our lives, and the way we talk will model this thinking. As well, the places we go will also be a reflection of this newfound revelation. Increase will always call for a new insight. Otherwise, your old mentality or mindset will draw you back into that "old" world.

Once your mind is expanded with new information about your status, you have to continue to "feed it" with additional truth in this area if you want to continue to grow in this area. I have already touched on this quite a bit in Chapter Two, but ruling in the business gate consistently will require constant upgrades. You don't want to become a liability for your own business.

Too many in the body of Christ are casualties within their own vision because of slothfulness to embrace change. Two years ago, I thought I was doing well. I have a home-based business and it had increased considerably. I am technical and computer literate. I am a part of all types of social media groups and networks, research a lot, so I thought I was doing well….until our PR & Marketing Consultant came and worked with me side-by-side in my office for an extended amount of time.

> *She said at my level of business and ministry, I could no longer just look the part, but I had to be a part.*

She brought several things to my attention. But the biggest was that my business/my company/my ministry/my office were technologically behind. She explained to me the place that God had me within in the business and ministry gate, and that I was in need of upgrading some things.

I had a cell phone, but it was not a smart phone. She explained that the caliber of business people I would be interfacing with will all have a smart phone. She said at my level of business and ministry, I could no longer just look the part, but I had to be a part.

You can't do business and ministry effectively when you don't have the right tools to do it with.

As well, communication is important in the business world and you must have every tool or resource, that which is mainstream, to communicate with people effectively. Before this, I looked at a cell phone just for emergencies and to make a few outgoing calls when the need arises. But, to be honest, I still prefer my cell phone be retained for outgoing calls instead of receiving a lot of incoming calls. Regardless, I needed to be able to text. Oh, by the way, she told me I needed to get a blue tooth, and I did.

Next, she realized I did not have a tablet to take notes on when traveling and in meetings, and all the other things you can do with a small device now. So, she researched tablets for me and I bought one. My laptop needed upgrading as well, it was freezing and taking 20 minutes sometimes to come up properly, so we had to buy one.

Then she saw all the things we will be doing as a business and ministry and we did not have any technology in place to capture these moments, so she found a very reasonable new camcorder camera for us to purchase. When she finished with me, I was technologically empowered. Even to the point, we had videos edited and uploaded to all of our websites.

You can't do business and ministry effectively when you don't have the right tools to do it with. Just recently, we purchased some more equipment we needed for our business and ministry: LCD projector, a banner and a screen. But God used our PR & Marketing Consultant to sow the seed in my life to move our business/ministry from looking like a liability or substandard entity to an established enterprise.

Also, I have gone through my entire house and assessed what is in my home. If it looked like I was living in a sub-standard mindset about something in my home, if I could throw it away, I did. You have to get rid of the old to embrace the new or make room for the new.

Millionaire Maker

"I have caused you to multiply as the bud of the field, and you have increased and become great, and you are come to excellent beauty: your breasts were formed, and your hair had grown, yet you were naked and bare." (Ezekiel 16:7)

> *The day you decide to become a millionaire, the universe will happily join the process and assist you in becoming a millionaire.*

I have caused you to multiply – In Hebrew, this statement means *"I have made you a million."* When I first heard a pastor say this is what this phrase meant, I said no way. Ok….here we go again, stretching the truth. Sarcastically, I said this to myself. So since I am a student of the Word, I noted it and said in the back of my mind I will check this out someday. But when God dropped in my spirit to start writing this book, on Easter Sunday morning, I began to quickly outline the chapters and some of the subtopics that I would be examining under each section; this came back to my memory.

I grabbed the book and DVD that I had originally heard and saw this and researched it. Boy, was I surprised.

When I actually saw it in the Hebrew commentary that it really said this, I started exclaiming and jumping around in my office. I could not believe what my eyes were reading -- *"I have made you a million."*

I knew I was going for "broke" then. Whatever it takes, this scripture will be fulfilled in my life before I leave this earth. I am going to **WORSHIP, PRAY and PRODUCE!**..until I reach God's desire for my life.

I am going to activate this word at its maximum level! Devil, it is on now.

When I began reading books about this subject by Christian millionaires, one of the things that was said that really "struck a cord" in my life was that the day you decide to become a millionaire, the universe will happily join the process and assist you in becoming a millionaire. I thought; "What an awesome statement!" I am going to be a true light bearer for God in more than what our traditional teaching teaches. I am going to be a financial example of the goodness of God. My company and I will be a great benefit and benefactor to the kingdom of God.

I have a girlfriend who makes over $6,000,000 dollars a year. God took her from making $19,000 a year to making over $6,000,000. God is able to do exceedingly abundantly above all we can ask or think.

Now, everywhere I go, I meet multi-millionaires. Just in one week, I communicated either on the phone or via email with three of them. Some of these millionaires have elevators in their homes. But the most substantial thing about these millionaires is that they are kingdompreneurs. They are millionaires that love God and give Him all the glory for what He has done in their lives.

They also know what their money is for – to help fund the gospel. One of my millionaire friends is writing a book called, "Holy Millionaire." It will be released in a soon. She said when she started making her millions; the bankers called her to arrange a meeting to meet with her. She did not know she could not keep a certain amount of money just sitting in a bank. They shared with her that she had to allot the money to go toward different things; basically, she had to do estate planning. She had no idea about this.

So as they were working with her to prepare her financial portfolio, they asked her where she wanted certain amounts of the money to go toward. She thought briefly, and then she said, "**The Bible said** that a good man should leave an inheritance for its children." So they set aside that amount for that. Then they asked her about another amount. She replied again, "**The Bible**

said we should provide for the widows and orphans." So they allotted that amount for that. Then they asked her about another amount. Her reply again, "**The Bible said** that we should give tithes and offerings unto the Lord." You see, this is a millionaire that knows who prospered her and what her money is for.

> *Wealth is a part of God's covenant to us. He is the One who gives us power to get wealth. He is the real millionaire maker.*

Wealth is a part of God's covenant to us. He is the One who gives us power to get wealth. He is the real millionaire maker.

"Who Wants to Become a Millionaire" is not just for a television program, it is for those of us who are covenant keeping people with Him. Prosperity is a sign of our covenant with God – *"I will rescue you and will make you* **both** *a* **symbol** *and a* **source** *of blessing"* (Zechariah 8:13 NLT). This millionaire friend of mine is both a symbol and a source.

What we have to grasp is that we are not subject to the times. God is not hindered by the world economy. We have been translated from the kingdom of curses (the devil) to the kingdom of blessings (God) – Colossians 1:13. Therefore, for us, the times are subject to the Word of God. We are under a different governing set of laws, so we have to think and act differently.

Even though there was a famine in the land during Isaac's era in Genesis, he continued to do what he had always done, he continued to sow. And because of this, he reaped a hundredfold in the **SAME** year.

To further clarify, let's look at what a famine is. Often we read over things in the Word of God, but to get an accurate picture of Isaac's situation, we need to know what a famine really is.

A famine is a *severe* shortage, *extreme* scarcity and a *serious* economic downturn. Notice the three words, severe, extreme and serious. All of these words represent something being very bad. For many of us, we have not experienced this type of hardship. Having your lights disconnected is not a famine. Not being able to pay your car note or your cell phone bill is not a famine. Everything suffers in a famine.

But what does the Word of God say to the body of Christ about times of famine:

*"They **will not** be disgraced in hard times; even in famine they will have more than enough."* (Psalm 37:18 NLT)

*"In times of disaster they **will not** wither; in days of famine they will enjoy plenty."* (Psalm 37:18 NIV)

*"He **will save** you from death in time of famine, from the power of the sword in time of war."* (Job 5:20 NLT).

We are not subject to the times. Even in the midst of extreme hardships, we can "find" God if we would stay our course. He said we will not be disgraced nor will we experience weakness or lack. So we must keep our focus and mental and emotional stamina in the midst of challenging and difficult times.

> *We are not subject to the times. Even in the midst of extreme hardships, we can "find" God if we would stay our course.*

But this is the real problem; we get out of alignment with Truth when hard times occur in our lives. How do I know, I have failed this test? It was only when I got back in alignment with the Word of God that things began to prosper in my life again. Whatever situation you are in now, and everything inside of you is telling you to compromise, **don't do it.** Stay the course, God will see you through it.

> *It was only when I got back in alignment with the Word of God that things began to prosper in my life again.*

SAY THIS WITH ME:

I am not moved by what I see

I am not moved by what I hear

I am going higher and

I am thriving and not just surviving

The Next Millionaires

This year, I had the privilege of reading a wonderful book by Paul Zane Pilzer title, **The Next Millionaires.** A friend told me about this book, and I will be forever grateful. This was one of the most powerful informative resource tools I had ever read. Paul is a New York Time Bestselling author and he is a Christian.

He is a professor and has been an economic advisor to two U. S. presidents and is a renowned world leading predictor of economic catalysts and trends. He has written several other books: **The Next Trillion, Unlimited Wealth and The Wellness Revolution.** His books are in 24 languages and he is a self-made millionaire. He made his first million before he was 26 and grossed over 10 million before he reached the age 30. His financial portfolio has credited him in starting

There are more than 547 millionaires created each day and 22.8 millionaires are created per hour. And less than 1 millionaire is created every sixty seconds.

and taking five companies public in the areas of software, education and financial services. So I think this qualifies him to speak on this subject.

He said in his book, in the ten years (1991-2001), the number of millionaire households doubled – from 3.6 million to 7.2 million. In the ten years (2006-2016), we will more than double this number. He predicts that there will be 10 million millionaires created with a total of 18.5 million millionaires. He called this **"The Millionaire Explosion."**

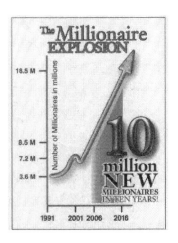

Graph from The Next Millionaires book

http://douglasvermeeren.wordpress.com/tag/how-many-millionaires-are-made-each-day/

A recent study by Dr. Jeffrey Rosenthal of the University of Toronto identified that in North America more than 200,000 people per year become millionaires. According to those numbers that would mean that there are more than 547 millionaires created each day and 22.8 millionaires are created per hour. And less than 1 millionaire is created every sixty seconds. It is possible for anyone with the vision and determination to achieve this attainable financial goal.

Anyone can become a millionaire in this age; we just have to understand the era we are living in.

Of course, being a millionaire doesn't necessarily mean you have millions of dollars in cash lying around your mansion and stuffed in the glove box of your Ferrari. To determine someone's overall wealth, all their holdings are looked at, including investments, cash, furniture, baseball cards, expensive automobiles, and real estate. However, a person's primary residence does not count toward the total.

But, regardless, anyone can become a millionaire in this age; we just have to understand the era we are living in. We are in a technology age, and the way to financial success is not manufacturing any longer. While this is a value entity in the world economy, but distribution should be our focus now. Rich people are into distribution not creation. People who found better ways of distributing things versus better ways of making things are the ones making the millions.

He mentioned such companies as Wal-Mart. How the secret to Sam Walton's success is distribution not manufacturing. In 1990, not only was Wal-Mart the largest retailer in the world, Sam Walton was also the richest person in the world. How did he do this – *distributing things other people made?*

Jeff Bezo, the founder of Amazon.com, did this as well. He is credited for revolutionizing the distribution of books. He is one of the newest entrepreneurs in our generation with a net worth now over 4.3 billion. Amazon.com does not actually distribute books to your door when you buy them; they have contracts with UPS and FedEX to do this. What did Jeff do? He found a better way to distribute books to you, the consumer.

This is also the same scenario with Pierre Omidyar, the founder of Ebay and Paypal. He is also touted as surpassing the physical distribution billionaires of yesterday.

So, where will the next millionaires come from — *from those who know how to get things to people better?* But this is just one "leg" to the journey.

Going forward, education will also have to be a part of the equation. We know this to be true because when we want to know something about a person, thing or subject, we don't have to physically leave our home and go to the library or bookstore any longer to buy or check out a book to find information out about this person, thing or subject, all we do now is "Google" it. So now not only is distribution important to us, information is equally important. Making the two primary "legs" of success going forward will be: education and distribution.

> *The next millionaires will be those who create new and better ways to educate consumers about products and services that will improve their lives.*

But Paul also predicts that the education component will eventually overshadow the distribution component.

However, this projection is mainly based on intellectual distribution. He said:

> *"When I wrote Unlimited Wealth in 1990, I predicated this physical distribution boom that would dominate the 1990s. But now the bulk of that boom has come and gone; the fortunes to be made there are mostly already made. The fortunes to be made in the years ahead will be predominately not in delivery but in education —not in physical distribution, but in intellectual distribution: educating consumers about products and services that will improve their lives...**but that they didn't yet know existed."***

Therefore, the next millionaires will be those who create new and better ways to educate consumers about products and services that will improve their lives. "The idea that most people inherit wealth is outdated. A lot is built through businesses, and business creation is the No. 1 driver of wealth in this country" according to one business writer.

Bottom line: Technology is changing constantly and rapidly. New products are at the forefront of this ever evolving change -- products that can drastically change and improve our lives or livelihood. Those who stand to make the fortune here are *those who can tell consumers about this technology or product first. Remember, 90% of all millionaires are made on the internet.*

If what you just read is not enough to get you energized to go after your million, then perhaps, the statistical report below will cajole you to change. Out of 100 people who worked from age 20 to age 65, this was their financial outcome.

BOTTOM 95%	TOP 5%
5 Still Working	4 Financially Independent
28 Dead	1 Rich
62 Dead Broke	

Taken from *"From Trash Man to Cash Man"* book.

Hopefully, after you read these statistics, you made up your mind to challenge your lifestyle and mindset to do things differently.

Wealth and the World

It is true as a nation, America; we are truly blessed. When compared to other countries and the overall world, our opportunities in America to excel are extremely greater. As stated previously, there are more than 547 millionaires created each day in America. These types of odds of someone becoming a millionaire in many countries are not available. However, what we call millionaires in America just might be called billionaires and trillionaires in some countries.

Just recently, I was introduced to the Global Rich List website. It is a global comparison money gauge that allows you to see where you stand or would stand financially if you made a certain amount of money within a year.

When I first started working with this chart, I was appalled how so little money made in a year, in America that for many countries it classified us as being rich. For example: If we had an annual income of $850, we were classified as being in the top 50% of the richest people in the world. If we made $1500 a year, we were classified as being in the top 24.8% of the richest people in the world. If we made $50,000 annually, we would be in the top 0.98% of the richest people in the world. Take a look at the next three pages and you will see it for yourself.

Global RichList

HOW RICH ARE YOU?

Every year we gaze enviously at the lists of the richest people in world. Wondering what it would be like to have that sort of cash. But where would you sit on one of those lists? Here's your chance to find out.

Just enter your annual income into the box below and hit 'show me the money'

MY ANNUAL INCOME $ US ▸   [850]   [Show me the money!]

Your RichList Position

= 3,000,000,001

You are the 3,000,000,001 richest person in the world!

You're in the TOP 50% richest people in the world!

◀— POOREST ——— THE WHOLE POPULATION OF THE WORLD! ——— RICHEST —▶

YOU
↓

Global Richlist

HOW RICH ARE YOU?

Every year we gaze enviously at the lists of the richest people in world. Wondering what it would be like to have that sort of cash. But where would you sit on one of those lists? Here's your chance to find out.

Just enter your annual income into the box below and hit 'show me the money'

MY ANNUAL INCOME

$ US ▼   1500   Show me the money!

Your RichList Position

= **1,488,503,335**   You're in the TOP 24.8% richest people in the world!

You are the 1,488,503,335 richest person in the world!

←— POOREST

YOU

——— THE WHOLE POPULATION OF THE WORLD! ———   RICHEST —→

Global RichList

HOW RICH ARE YOU?

Every year we gaze enviously at the lists of the richest people in world. Wondering what it would be like to have that sort of cash. But where would you sit on one of those lists? Here's your chance to find out.

Just enter your annual income into the box below and hit 'show me the money'

MY ANNUAL INCOME | $ US ▾ | 50,000 | Show me the money!

Your RichList Position

= 59,029,289

You are the 59,029,289 richest person in the world!

You're in the TOP 0.98% richest people in the world!

YOU →

◄— POOREST ———————— THE WHOLE POPULATION OF THE WORLD! ———————— RICHEST —►

Wow, these figures are starling. I wonder how so many people can do without so much of the amenities that we have in America.

Why did I share this? Because so often we look to others in America to define our greatness, when in actuality, we are already tremendously blessed from a global standpoint? Also, hopefully, this will be some point of reference when we begin to talk about true riches of this world. Of course, you should know by now, I am not advocating that anyone be poor or live like a meager, but I want to make sure that we keep a right perspective when addressing money. Furthermore, I hope you were blessed by this chart like I was. No wonder so many people are trying to come to America.

What Are You Worth?

If you are going to make it as a successful entrepreneur, then you have to know your worth. If you don't, you will wind up like me for many years making very little money for all my efforts. A lot of this was due to the fact I was trying to be a blessing to the body of Christ. Don't get me wrong, there is nothing wrong with blessing God's people, but we have to make sure we don't fall into the trap of devaluing our lives and services.

One thing I learned was that "church folks" are always looking for you to work something out for them or work a deal out. Because I did this, I made very little money for my efforts. Constantly, there was a perpetual cycle of people wanting to work a deal out.

> *Every time I worked out a deal and/or gave someone a favor, I was ultimately devaluing my services. I like what the Psychologist and television host, Dr. Phil McGraw says about this, "We tell people how to treat us."*

In the long run, I realized it was my mistake. Every time I worked out a deal and/or gave someone a favor, I was ultimately devaluing my services. I like what the Psychologist and television host, Dr. Phil McGraw says about this, "We tell people how to treat us." And this is exactly what I had done. I told people to pay me little. This is why I only drew people to me that had that type of mentality – get over, wanting a favor or wanting to work something out.

The type of work we did with book publication was quite tedious and required a lot of time in editing. But my prices did not reflect this. As time went on, we realized the people did not know how much work went into the process nor did they understand the value of what we were doing for them. Because of this, I, at times, felt quite frustrated at their attitudes. Finally, enough was enough.

I told God I wanted to attract people to my business that understood commerce. I did not want any more just "church folks," but people in the body of Christ that had an enterprising mentality and spirit. I took a stand that I would no longer devalue me or my services. When I did this, God blessed.

You see, as long as I was devaluing me and my services, I attracted people that thought the same way.

Immediately, He began to give me clientele that mirrored my request. The first was a former news reporter for a major local television station. The second person owned a whole block downtown. And by the way, my prices went up into the thousands. I am so ashamed of what I was charging before that I will never put it in writing.

You see, as long as I was devaluing me and my services, I attracted people that thought the same way. You have to know what you and your services are worth if you are going to be successful in business, and don't be afraid to charge a certain amount.

Now, when people ask me about my prices, I let them know that our prices are comparable to those in the same industry. And that we customize all of our packages according to our clients' needs and that we will be more than happy to speak with them extensively about their needs, then prepare a couple of options that perhaps can help them achieve their desired goal. Since we have established this protocol, our business has tripled.

Most of what we do for our clients is done from a strategic standpoint. What we do is that we come along aside our clients and assist them in creating the finances they need to pay for our services. We coach them, we open up doors of opportunities for them, we literally connect the missing dots in their lives, so that we can properly brand and market them. We have a motto in our book publication service – *"We just don't create authors, we raise up entrepreneurs."*

Financial Empowerment Exercise

As I close out this section, I want to share with you one of the empowerment exercises some of the millionaires shared that they did to provoke an *initial* substantial change in their financial situation. They said on a CD that I was listening to that if you would do this 90 days, your financial situation would change drastically.

Well, I was not where I wanted to be financially, and I wanted a tsunami change in my finances. I had heard several millionaires say they did this, so I thought what did I have to lose. I had everything to gain, nothing to lose.

For 90 days, I did this exercise. After 90 days, my income increased considerably.

So I submit this to you; hoping prayerfully, that you will take this to heart if your financial situation needs to be shifted. I wholeheartedly encourage you to try it.

1. Read 15 to 20 minutes every day motivational or uplifting information -- Read materials that strengthen your mind and bring value to your life.

2. Cut off your TV – Do not watch TV, especially the news. The news brings disempowerment information. However, you can watch uplifting DVDs.

3. Turn off your radio – Eliminate disempowerment information. Listen to **ONLY** empowering and uplifting information. Make your automobile a moving university.

4. Newspaper – Do not read the newspaper. Don't cancel your subscription if you have one, just don't read it. Most information in newspapers is disempowerment information.

5. Associate with empowering people – If you need to, add more empowering and uplifting people into your equation. Sometimes you can't get rid of all of the negative people in your life, but you can minimize the amount of time you spend with negative disempowering people.

6. Drink plenty of water – Some people don't do better just because they just don't feel good.

7. Exercise – Exercise 20 minutes each day. It will energize you and help your overall physically.

8. Reflect - Take 15 to 20 minutes to be reflective. Think about the things you have learned that day. Think happy thoughts, not negative thoughts.

Now listen, I recognized everything on this list is easy. But because it is easy, we often have a tendency not to do it. You have to ask yourself, how bad do you want change. If you want it bad enough then you will follow through. It is said we are either going to do the simple disciplines in life or make the simple errors in judgment. I personally wanted change bad enough that I followed through no matter what. Some nights at 9 p.m., I had to walk around my house just to get my exercise in. The race is not given to the swift, but to he that endures to the end.

There is much more I can say on this subject, but let me conclude with this. One of the startling things I discovered in my reading that so many of us really don't ask God for what we really want. We say things like, "Lord, I want a job that I can make $50,000 a year," or "Lord, I want a six-figure job," but in actuality, you really want more than this.

> *Rich people don't ask or talk about obtaining or finding a job, they talk about ways to increase their income.*

So let me direct you here to help you start creating a millionaire mindset.

First of all: If you want to become a millionaire, ask God to help you. You can say something like this: *"Lord, I need your help to help me to become a millionaire, so I can bless Your kingdom – become a distribution center for You."* Some go on to say, you need to confess that you are already a millionaire. If this is you, go for it. We just need your verbiage to acknowledge what your *real* desire is.

Second: Daily you need to ask the big question: "How Do I Earn or Create a Million Dollars?"

Thirdly: Rich people don't ask or talk about obtaining or finding a job, they talk about ways to increase their income. They are about increasing their net worth – their wealth.

Conduct and Character with Money

As God is moving His body into places of authority in the economic mountain throughout the world, we have to "play" by another set of rules. These rules are not the customary cut throat, "dog eat dog" rules that are paramount in corporate America. These are rules governed by the Word of God.

Our way(s) of doing business has a higher character calling and an anointing of grace. It is important that we address this issue and outline that which is expected because the climate in corporate America has a tendency to make you believe that you have to do business this way or you won't be successful.

> *Our way(s) of doing business has a higher character calling and an anointing of grace.*

Those of us who are called to rule in marketplace ministry, we must know what God is requiring of us. To begin this discourse, let's look at Proverbs 1:3 in the New Living Translation:

"Their purpose is to teach people to live disciplined and successful lives, to help them do what is right, just, and fair."

We have to be honest people if we want perpetual blessings to flow in our lives.

The writings of Proverbs by King Solomon were written for the purpose to teach us to live a disciplined and successful life, so that we might help others to do what is right, just and fair. I think it will be fair to say, if we are going to teach others to be right, just and fair, then we have to be right, just and fair. Therefore, in our business dealings in order to maintain our success; we must be disciplined and honest people.

Our first character checkpoint is honesty. This is the overall takeaway from this scripture. We have to be honest people if we want perpetual blessings to flow in our lives. When the Early Church was in need of deacons to be installed in the church to assist with administrative tasks, the twelve disciples instructed the church to look for seven men of honest report (Acts 6:3). Not someone that was dishonest and greedy, but people of character. So if you lack character in this area now, this is a good time to start working on it. Don't wait till you get money because money will only magnify what is in your heart. If your heart is diseased, your money will be diseased. If your heart is right, then your money will be right.

Next, let's look at I Timothy 6:10, 17-19:

<u>King James Version:</u> *For the love of money is the root of all evil: which while some coveted after, they have erred from the faith, and pierced themselves through with many sorrows. (vs. 10)*

<u>International Standard Version:</u> *For the love of money is a root of all kinds of evil. Some people, in their eagerness to get rich, have wandered away from the faith and caused themselves a lot of pain. (vs. 10)*

<u>GOD'S WORD Translation:</u> *Certainly, the love of money is the root of all kinds of evil. Some people who have set their hearts on getting rich have wandered away from*

the Christian faith and have caused themselves a lot of grief. (vs. 10)

"Command those who are rich in this present age not to be haughty, nor to trust in uncertain riches but in the living God, who gives us richly all things to enjoy. Let them do good, that they be rich in good works, ready to give, willing d time to come, that they may lay hold on eternal life."(vs. 17-19)

Verse 10: *The Love of money is the root of all evil*

Money is not evil, but a greedy and lustful spirit about attaining wealth is. We should not love money, we should love God. If we spend all of our time chasing money our latter end will be ruin – *"...Some people who have set their hearts on getting rich have wandered away from the Christian faith and have caused themselves a lot of grief."*

Verse 17: *Not to trust in riches*

We don't trust money, we trust God. *"Some trust in chariots and some in horses, but we trust in the name of the LORD our God."* (Psalm 20:7 NIV).

Verse 18: *We should be givers*

We should be givers not takers. We are distributor centers for God. Don't ever forget that our purpose for accumulation is distribution.

Finally, let's look at Matthew 6:24:

"No man can serve two masters: for either he will hate the one, and love the other; or else he will hold to the one, and despise the other. Ye cannot serve God and mammon."

We are called to serve God and not money. When we are blessed financially, we have to be careful that we don't become enslaved to money. Money can become a trap, an emotional prison if we don't keep money in its right perspective.

Money serves us, we serve God!

Blessings Blockers

There are so many scriptures and variables in the Word of God that governs money. Some share how we should think about money. Others share how we should act with money. While there are some who share what we should do with money; but there are also especially a plethora of scriptures that warns us of the mishandling and/or misappropriating of money in our lives.

> *If you are going to change your financial portfolio, you have to think differently when spending money.*

Because of all of these variables, we want to address these detractors as well as how they will affect our financial success portfolio if we don't alleviate these things out of our financial dealings. And for sake of training and teaching, we are going to call them blessings blockers.

If we don't conquer or successfully alleviate these things in and out of our lives, we will forever be hindered in our financial growth. And instead of moving forward, these areas will serve as an obstruction for our financial advancement.

Now, let's look at these blessings blockers:

- <u>Being a Consumer Versus Being a Producer</u>

In one of the books I read, it said if we are not making $25,000 month, we need to throw our television away. I know this might sound quite drastic to some, but what the author shared in the book was that television is set up to entice you to spend money frivolously so that you can become more a consumer and not a producer. All the commercials on television are not being shown so you can say how nice they are. No, they are there to encourage you to buy a product or service. And they do a good job at it.

Large corporations spend billions of dollars a year on television commercials. The reason they continue to do this is that it works. We consume their goods, services and/or products. We buy them.

However, if you are going to change your financial portfolio, you have to think differently when spending money. Here is a rule to help you monitor what you should be spending your money on. Is what you are spending your money on number one, bringing value to your life, and/or number two, is what you spending your money on a resource to increase your financial holdings. If it does not align with these two criteria, then don't buy it.

A millionaire by the name of Johnny Wimbrey has a free training booklet that he gives to those who sign up to be on his mailing list called, *"The 7 Secrets to Becoming a Million Dollar Producer."* He said over the years, he has studied his own success as well as the success of other millionaires, celebrities, athletes, entrepreneurs, four-star generals, world leaders, and people from all walks of life who are producers. He said out of his investigation, he discovered seven characteristics that distinguished these successful people from the masses of unsuccessful people.

Now, in this booklet, he compared them to procrastinators. Even so, I believe what he has said still connects with our theme in this section. On the next page are the seven characteristics he identified:

1. Producers are winners, not whiners

2. Producers respond, not react

3. Producers are optimistic, not pessimistic

4. Producers take a risk, not make a wish

5. Producers have vision, not illusion

6. Producers prepare, not improvise

7. Producers execute, not make excuses

As you can see, this is a wonderful list to add to our consideration "box" when spending money and moving toward increasing our financial worth. Let's become more producers instead of consumers.

Also, don't let setbacks stop you from being producers. No matter what season we are encountering in our lives, a product can be produced out of that season. So you're going through a bad time now financially. Sitting around doing nothing will not change your situation. But "working" on you, will. Bring value to your life by increasing your worth by reading more about your situation on Google and research possible solutions. In your process of doing this, what's going to happen is that you are going to find yourself becoming more solution conscious than problem conscious. By your "psyche" shifting to this role, the cosmic world will begin to create new doors of opportunities for you.

It is said that if you can eat it or wear it, don't put it on your credit card.

You see, in tough times you have to keep your head up. Believe it or not chaos can breed opportunities. So stay still to what you know and articulate your ideas clearly to what you want to do - going forward.

- Debt

It is said that if you can eat it or wear it, don't put it on your credit card. I love this, and this is why I am an advocate for the most part **against** consumer credit card use. It is my experience with credit cards that brought me to this resolve. Trying to live the American dream, my family ended up in an enormous amount of debt. Now, we are out from under all of this debt and as my family was coming out of this situation I began to assess how we got into the mess we were in, and mainly I realized we believe that the credit card companies had our back. Nothing was farther than the truth. They had **"their"** back.

Now, I know for some things in this world go better with using credit cards. However, you can use a debit card like a credit card. The only challenge I have ever had with this is that when I was traveling, I did not always have a surplus of money in the bank to cover the extra money that rental cars and hotels would hold against your money in the bank until the bill was finalized. So in my transitional financial increase state, I applied for a credit card to cover these rentals and accommodations when traveling. The key here is to pay it off immediately.

It usually takes two days for these companies sometimes to finalize everything and release your money, but after it is finalized, go online and pay the balance off. Do not spend this money. Pay it off that week. Don't wait for the bill in the mail, pay it off immediately. If not, you are going into debt.

Remember, debt holds you back. It reduces cash flow for other things, including investing. Some say if no one gave us money to borrow, we would be better off and the economy would be smaller.

> *Remember, debt holds you back. It reduces cash flow for other things, including investing.*

Still not convinced? Then, let's see what the Word says since this should be our ultimate authority in our lives.

Romans 13:8: "Owe no man anything, but to love one another: for he that loves another has fulfilled the law."

The Amplified Version says, "**Keep out of debt** *and* owe no man anything, except to love one another; for he who loves his neighbor [who practices loving others] has fulfilled the Law.

Please notice the words "keep out." These words mean refrain from; stay away from; don't do it. These are pretty powerful words. Listen, we make up a lot of reasons why we use credit cards, but overall the banks that finance credit cards are not doing this for us. They are purely doing this for their own selfish reasons and desires. It's a business opportunity for them. Some of their practices have changed because so many people have had to default on their credit card bills, but it is truly a business transaction.

If you are in debt right now, you want to empower yourself with information. Some of the best materials available now are Dave Ramsey's Financial Peace University. It helped my family out tremendously. Trust me, I had read quite a bit of information about personal finances for years, and it got to a point that everything I was reading was regurgitating the same information I had read numerous times. So when I was talking with a friend one day about Dave Ramsey, I immediately "shut her down." In all of my research, nobody had any new relevant information that was practical enough that got us out of our situation. So when my friend started talking to me about Dave Ramsey, I told her I did not want to hear it. She said, Shirley, this is different. I said okay sarcastically...but God knew my heart.

My friend had just had the opportunity to hear Dave Ramsey at our church. He came through our area and his business rented our event facility. My husband is a sound engineer, and at this time, worked as a part-time contractual service engineer for our church. This particular event, he was asked to work. When he came home, he had practically everything of Dave Ramsey. So one day as I was heading to my car to go somewhere I was led to take the CDs with me.

When you are in debt, you are a slave to the lender.

When I got in the car, I looked at all the titles, and they definitely piqued my interest, so I began listening to them in my comings and goings. I could not believe what I was hearing. Finally, all the answers to all of my questions were being answered. I felt soooo empowered as a consumer that I knew God was doing something inside of me. I knew my financial situation was getting ready to change.

I cannot tell you the release and peace I had after listening to Dave Ramsey's CDs. I will be forever grateful to Dave Ramsey. Within two years, my husband and I were out of about a $100,000 worth of debt except for our home. Thanks, Dave Ramsey. We are truly a fan.

As I close out this topic, let me say this, and I am sure many of you have heard this before, but it is still true. When you are in debt, you are a slave to the lender.

Proverbs 22:7 (NIV) says it this way, *"The rich rule over the poor, **and the borrower is slave to the lender.**"*

- Financial Illiteracy

It is said what you don't know financially, it is being used against you. I truly believe this today more than ever after what my family went through with debt. When you are being wooed and sucked into this invisible web of debt that entangled you, you can't see what is happening at the moment. And the reason we are so oblivious to this whole process is that we are financially illiterate or our financial knowledge base is too limited.

You see, I had read much material about personal finance, but I never saw the whole picture. So I didn't understand the banking system nor did I know truly why I was pre-approved to receive credit cards. Again, I would like to thank Dave Ramsey for this enlightened information. Do you know if you "bounce" a check at your bank this week, most likely, you will be flooded with credit card offers almost immediately?

Why is this? Because they know you might be from time to time challenged in paying your credit card bill, therefore, they can charge not just interest, but late fees. They are depending on you to fail. Did you hear me, they want you to fail. Banks make no money from you paying your bills on time when it comes to consumer debts. According to Dave Ramsey, years ago, banks made over **90 billion dollars** on bank fees and penalties that they charged us. This is outrageous!!!

We cannot afford to be financially illiterate any longer. When we don't know how systems work, then we will forever get the "short end of the stick." The banking industry is a business. We salute this industry, but we don't have to fund this industry at least not with our hard earned money. So I recommend from this day forward that you begin to educate yourself in the various genres (banking, personal, savings, investment, etc.) in the financial world. It will definitely enrich your life and empower you to make better decisions about money.

- Slothfulness

The best way to start this discourse is a quote from the book of Proverbs, Chapter 13 and Verse 4, *"Lazy people want much but get little, but those who work hard will prosper"* (New Living Translation). If you are lazy, you will get little.

I love the book of Proverbs how it deals with a lazy person versus a diligent man. It is so clear to me that if I am striving to achieve greatness in my life for the kingdom of God, then I have to give God something to work with.

God wants to empower our lives so we can do great things for Him, but we must be diligent servants.

Two of my favorite scriptures that I have written down on my vision boards in my office are Proverbs 22:29 and Proverbs 10:4. The first ones say, *"Seest thou a man diligent in his business? He shall stand before kings; he shall not stand before mean men."* This scripture is so good; I want you to see it in other translations. It is so powerful!

New International Version
Do you see someone skilled in their work? They will serve before kings; they will not serve before officials of low rank.

New Living Translation
Do you see any truly competent workers? They will serve kings rather than working for ordinary people.

English Standard Version
Do you see a man skillful in his work? He will stand before kings; he will not stand before obscure men.

Holman Christian Standard Bible
Do you see a man skilled in his work? He will stand in the presence of kings. He will not stand in the presence of unknown men.

International Standard Version
Do you see a man skilled in his work? He will work for kings, not unimportant people.

God wants to empower our lives so we can do great things for Him, but we must be diligent servants. Many of us want to stand or be known by "great" people, but the path to this greatness is being diligent in that which God has called us to do. God will not bless slothfulness.

Achieving increase in your finances has not just to do with your knowledge base, but with also who you know.

Also, Proverbs 10:4 says, *"Lazy hands make for poverty, but diligent hands bring wealth"* (NIV). This scripture is self-explanatory. If you want to be poor, be lazy. If you want to be wealthy, then you have to work. You have to be consistently involved in the process. *"The rich man's wealth is his strong city: the destruction of the poor is their poverty"* (Proverbs 10:15).

- <u>Wrong Connections</u>

Achieving increase in your finances has not just to do with your knowledge base, but with also who you know. You have to be properly connected or aligned with the right people when trying to increase wealth in your life. Why is this so important?

Association breeds assimilation. Therefore, the more you are with wealthy people, the more you will acquire a higher level of thinking about money, power, influence and success.

Association breeds assimilation. Therefore, the more you are with wealthy people, the more you will acquire a higher level of thinking about money, power, influence and success. Plus, the atmosphere and mindsets that exult from the cosmic energy that these types of individuals release will "spill" over on you. And this is exactly what you are after and want.

Sometimes it can be simple things like this that is hindering our continuous prosperity. I met a lady recently while ministering out of town who told me how her family was rich, millionaires to be exact, but she said, throughout her life she would get money, but she couldn't keep money. It seemed as though something was always taking her money from her. There were holes in her pockets, and she could not secure or fortify these holes.

Second, at times, she had been giving $100,000 dollars or more, but it would always wind up being depleted. She did not know why, but she knew it was a problem. She was very adamant about me understanding that she could create or draw money, but it would always "leave" her. I did not have the time to fully assess her situation, but sometimes the problem can be as simple as your associations.

What you must realize is that money speaks and has a voice. It is a silent voice, but yet powerful! I read once in a book about associations. It said:

- ❖ You will never be bigger than the associations you keep

- ❖ You will be known as much for the people you avoid as the ones that you associate with

- ❖ The associations you permit will yield the results you have to live with

Now, the Bible says it this way: *"Be not deceived: evil communications corrupt good manners"* (I Corinthians 15:33).

You want to begin to associate with people with like minds. Otherwise, you will not get overall the results you want in the long run with your financial portfolio.

- <u>Co-Signing For Others</u>

Co-signing for others to get loans or to serve as a surety for someone's utility to be turned on is a failure model. It is a poor judgment decision. I have fallen into this trap as I thought it was my "Christian" duty. I was young in the Lord and I believe these people knew it. They knew I was vulnerable and basically they took advantage of my youthfulness and zeal. To this day, I remember seeing a smirk or some "get over" spirit on this person's face, but I ignored it. I was excited and wanted to be a "good" Christian. What I did not know was what the Bible said about this.

"My child, if you have put up security for a friend's debt or agreed to guarantee the debt of a stranger, if you have trapped yourself by your agreement and are caught by what you said. Follow my advice and save yourself, for you have placed yourself at your friend's mercy" (Proverbs 6:1-3NLT).

Here's the thing, the bank or utility company has already deemed this person not worthy to be invested in. They are too much of a risk for them. So if they are too much of a risk for them, then they are definitely too much of a risk for you. You will always lose co-signing for someone.

The real issue here is character. This person has done things in the past and/or just not qualified to receive this amount of credit or financing. As I stated earlier, I did this for someone and guess what, I got stuck paying the bill.

- Lack of Proper Counseling

In the book of Proverbs, it says where there is no counsel, purpose is disappointed. Sitting under tutors and counselors is a must especially when God begins to bless you financially.

> *Sitting under tutors and counselors is a must especially when God begins to bless you financially.*

Never assume you have arrived. Remember, your destination is a journey. And it is constantly laced with obstacles and unknown as well as unwanted detractors.

It is said that everyone needs an advisor, a mentor, a sponsor and now, a coach. According to a Wall Street Executive, we mostly can do without three of these people, but if we are going to move up financially, we have to have a sponsor. She said we can survive without a mentor, a coach and advisor, but not a without a sponsor. She said the thing that the sponsor has over all of these other people is that the sponsor has a seat at the table. Behind closed doors this person can carry your agenda into a meeting and can use his or her political influence to favor you.

You might be asking Dr. Clark, what is the difference between these individuals? Glad you asked. Here are the definitions:

❖ **An Advisor** – An advisor is someone you can ask discreet questions to

❖ **A Mentor** -- A person you tell everything to (the good, the bad, and the ugly)

❖ **A Sponsor** -- A person with incredible influence that sits at the table with the other decision-makers and major influencers

❖ **A Coach** – A coach is someone who encourages you and helps you navigate through the turbulence and transitional times in your life as well as assists you with your hands-on personal and professional developmental growth.

Proverbs 15:22 says:

New International Version
Plans fail for lack of counsel, but with many advisers they succeed.

New Living Translation
Plans go wrong for lack of advice; many advisers bring success.

English Standard Version
Without counsel plans fail, but with many advisers they succeed.

New American Standard Bible
Without consultation, plans are frustrated, But with many counselors they succeed.

King James Bible
Without counsel purposes are disappointed: but in the multitude of counsellers they are established.

As you can see, it is important that we have a multitude of credible integral group of people around us to assist us in our financial elevation. Get rid of the "lone ranger" spirit today because you are going to need someone to help guide you through some things in this world.

I have an incredible group of individuals around me that can speak into my life about various subjects, but I am still adding more into my equation. I have set up a system of success for me in this area. Many on my counseling support council are millionaires. This was done deliberately, and of course, the grace of God made all these connections come to pass as I sought HIM that these people would embrace and allow me to come into their personal space.

When you have a higher level of support council or people that operate in another level of financial freedom they are familiar with more options than perhaps you are.

If there is something I am doing that is "out of my league," you better believe it, I will be on the phone in a hurry with one of these individuals soliciting their insight and guidance.

I don't like wasting time, so if I can save time in the beginning, this is what I want to do. I don't like re-inventing the wheel if the wheel is already there. A lot of times, when we are moving up we don't always know that certain things are already in place or in existence because we have never been in that place before. But when you have a higher level of support council or people that operate in another level of financial freedom they are familiar with more options than perhaps you are. It is just a given that money allows you to have more options, which can actually open up another world for you.

Don't allow anyone (preachers, your family members, etc.) talk you out of your prophetic inheritance.

As I sat with my girlfriend, who is worth over six million dollars now, she shared how her world changed drastically when she started making millions. So many doors and opportunities were availed to her. Things she had never heard of before were being presented to her. I thank God for her every day because I know she is rooting for my success and financial elevation. So please build a strong financial support team that can help you navigate through life's many ups and downs.

- <u>Wrong Teaching</u>

Wrong teaching about finance in your life can impair, hinder and can even bring you to financial ruin. I am adamantly against any teaching that says God wants us poor. Somebody has to finance the gospel – it just makes sense! We cannot give to the kingdom of God or kingdom endeavors if we are broke. Somebody has to have the resources that we can receive funding from. So the teaching that God wants us poor does not line up with the support and distribution plan of God for kingdom endeavors – *"But you shall remember the LORD your God: for it is he that gives you power to get wealth, that he may establish his covenant which he swore unto your fathers, as it is this day."* Another translation says He gives us power to **produce** wealth. God wants to establish His kingdom on this earth. And much of this will be fulfilled when we own the silver, gold and the land.

Don't allow anyone (preachers, your family members, etc.) talk you out of your prophetic inheritance. You are the seed of Abraham and Abraham was blessed beyond measure. Believe God for your inheritance and receive it today! God wants you blessed not broke!!!

• <u>Limited Skill-Sets</u>

The ability to exercise authority in another level or dimension will always be congruent with the level of preparation that precedes this elevation. Preparation is always the doorway or gateway to transition. Where you are today is a determining factor of your preparation stage in the past. So your today is a picture of past aspirations and your tomorrow will be a manifested vision of your today's thoughts and actions.

Therefore, if you want your tomorrow to be an expression of something that can be lauded, then **today** you must create a "world" that will elicit your desired outcome. Basically, you have to prepare for your shift. So often we want certain things to happen in our lives, but we have aborted our own dreams and visions by not doing what it would take to achieve these goals. With this being said, sometimes we might have to go back to school and get some additional training so that we can master a skill. There is nothing wrong with being the best.

Having limited skill-sets is a too easy problem to solve. There are many opportunities and avenues whereby we can receive advancement training in numerous subject areas. Internet has opened up the entire world to us and pretty much you can learn everything online. We have no excuse now for being ignorant and unlearned. The internet provided for all an even playing field.

> *Technology is changing constantly and in order for us to be relevant, we must position ourselves to change with it.*

Technology is changing constantly and in order for us to be relevant, we must position ourselves to change with it. This is what I love about the story of Daniel in the book of Daniel, Chapter One. It talks about how Daniel was in a heathen land, but even though he was in a foreign land in captivity, he was relevant to the times and he was considered wise and skillful – *"Then the king commanded Ashpenaz,* *his chief eunuch, to bring some of the people of Israel, both of the royal family and of the nobility, youths without blemish, of good appearance and **skillful in all wisdom, endowed with knowledge, understanding learning, and competent to stand in the king's palace, and to teach them the literature and language of the Chaldeans"** (Daniel 1:4).

The best way to get yourself ready for increase is preparation. You have to make room for the new by dismantling the old. If not, you will be forever operating from your past experiences and history. Life is about going forward, not backward. It is about progression and regression.

As I stated earlier, you don't want to be a liability for your own vision.

Chapter Five

The Empowered Life

"If they listen and serve him, they'll finish their lives in prosperity and their years will be pleasant."

Job 36:11 (ISV)

As believers, if we are obeying the Word of God, then we should be living under an opened heaven. The Word of God says He will open up the windows of heaven and pour us out a blessing we will not have room enough to receive it (Malachi 3:12).

For those of us who are tithers and givers in the house of the Lord, this is a wonderful promise for our commitment to obedience. In another translation this scripture says, I will open the windows of heaven and flood you with blessing after blessing. All of this is great, and certainly something to be excited about. But what I have noticed in the body of Christ is that many of us have mentally embraced this scripture, but in actuality we never live consistently under this opened heaven. Hopefully, as you read this chapter, and hear how God has blessed my life, you will be challenged to live under this open heaven, so that you might have an empowered life.

> *An empowered life is where your barns are always filled and overflowing and daily God loads you with benefits.*

It is my goal in this chapter to introduce to some and reinforce to others the concept of spending your days in prosperity – living from an Empowered Life. An empowered life is where your barns are always filled and overflowing and *daily* God loads you with benefits.

Psalms 68:19 says, *"Blessed be the Lord, who **daily** loads us with benefits, the God of our salvation!"*

In the Douay-Rheims Bible, it says, *"Blessed be the Lord **day by day**: the God of our salvation will make our journey prosperous to us."*

In Barnes' Notes on the Bible, it says, *"Blessed be the Lord, who daily loadeth us with benefits ...literally, **"day, day;"** that is, day by day; or, **constantly."***

And in Matthew 6:11, it says, *"Give us this day our **daily** bread."*

In Douay-Rheims Bible this scripture is *"Give us this day our supersubstantial bread."*

Finally in Job 36:11, it says, *"If they obey and serve him, they shall spend their days in prosperity, and their years in pleasures."* Complete Live out

The word *"spend"* in this scripture means complete, live out, accomplish and end his days in prosperity.

God wants us to finish strong in this life. He wants us to have an enjoyable life that prospers while serving Him. He wants our lives to be empowered with His goodness at all times. The Psalmist tells us that the righteous shall flourish like the palm tree and we should grow like a cedar in Lebanon.

According to a Bible commentary, it is said that the Cedar tree is one of the most aromatic and resistant types of wood known. And the variety known as the Cedar of Lebanon was said to be of especially good quality, solid, without many knots, and of a deep rich reddish color. These trees were unusual shaped and were quite wide with branches growing nearly straight out. They would grow as tall as 100 feet of more in height. Its very name symbolized strength and magnificence.

This is what an empowered life looks like. A life that is strong in the Lord and one with lots of depth. One that is unique and precious in the sight of God.

Miraculous Provisions

When we walk in an empowered life, miraculous provisions will be made available to us. It is the norm for those who are walking in an empowered life anointing to reap where they have not sown (Leviticus 25:11) and have houses we did not build (Deuteronomy 28). This is what an empowered life looks like. The supernatural will always be a part of a person's life that is walking in an empowered life anointing.

> *There is a frequency that I have released over my life that is constantly in agreement with where God is taking me.*

We will reap what we did not ask for (I King 3:13) and be given things that we did not work for (Isaiah 55:1). The miraculous will be a constant flow in an empowered person's life. In addition, we are forever favored in this empowered lifestyle – *"For his anger lasts only a moment,* **but his favor lasts a lifetime;** *weeping may stay for the night, but rejoicing comes in the morning."*

Notice this scripture says "lifetime." Not a month or two or a year, it says lifetime. This speaks volume to us regarding God's goodness and His heart for us to live abundantly. We have to read out of the scripture and not read into the scripture. So often we read over scriptures like this and casually think of this from a sporadic blessing standpoint. But this is not what this scripture says, it says lifetime. We have many promises in the Word of God, but they do not automatically operate in our lives. We have to activate faith in order to receive the promises of God. Therefore, to spend your days in prosperity and to be favored an entire lifetime, you must believe this word, begin to speak this word and expect it to operate in your life.

"For by me thy days shall be multiplied, and the years of thy life shall be increased)" (Proverbs 9:11).

I expect this to happen in my life and I activate this word through daily confessions and several other exercises that releases a creative environment for change. Some days I get so busy that I don't have enough time to do some of them, but my spirit "speaks" for me. There is a frequency that I have released over my life that is constantly in agreement with where God is taking me. I don't move from it. I don't sway from it. I don't flint about it. **IT IS A FACT FOR ME!**

When your life takes on an overflow dimension, wicked people will not be able to oppress you anymore.

This is why I don't spend much time with people because I must keep my spirit clean or clear of unwanted debris in this area. I know I have a higher level of mentality in this realm. If I talk too much to people sometimes they "invade" my thinking process, which requires me to step outside of my "world" I have created in the spirit.

You see, you have to protect the "garden" of your mind. Every negative interruption takes away from the positive energy in your life. I love living in peace, therefore, I will withdraw quickly from chaotic situations. If I am in charge, I make decisions quickly to eradicate negative environments. Your goal should be to do the same. You want to create a vortex that is filled with positive reinforcements in all areas of your life. By doing this, God (because He is peace) and the cosmic world will partner with your life to empower you. It is an incredible zone to live within. It's called living in the overflow.

Living in the Overflow

2 Samuel 7:10 says, *"And I will provide a place for my people Israel and will plant them so that they can have a home of their own and no longer be disturbed. Wicked people will not oppress them anymore, as they did at the beginning and have done ever since the time I appointed leaders over my people Israel. I will also give you rest from all your enemies."*

When your life takes on an overflow dimension, wicked people will not be able to oppress you anymore. You will live in peace and not be disturbed. Now, this does not mean that some negative things will not happen to you, but if they do, you will not be dismayed. It takes a renewed, transformed and reformed mind to understand and to fully encapsulate this dimension of living.

Most people have subjected their lives to the times. So they have a "worldly" mentality instead of a kingdom mentality. It really is a lifestyle. When it says in 3 John 2, that it wishes **ABOVE** all that we will prosper and be in good health **EVEN** as our soul prospers, this is a clarion call for us to live in the overflow. It is a standard. If we prosper our soul, we are guaranteed to live in the overflow.

Recording artist, Grace Williams has a soaking CD called, **"Overflow,"** which happens to be a featured song on the CD. I encourage you today to download and create a playlist of the entire CD on your media and/or spotify player.

I listen to this song and CD over and over again. As soon as I hear the music, the Holy Spirit shows up instantly and I am empowered to do and acquire more.

What am I doing? Why do my atmosphere change when I put this song on? Because it prophesy to my prophetic destiny of wealth and it releases manifestations. And it is in these manifestations that information, wealth, resources and favor are release.

You see; if you are going to reap these benefits. You have to believe. And you have to believe with all your heart. Everything inside of you must believe it. **Wish above all** – this statement truly will make you the head and not the tail.

Here is one of the abundant overflow affirmations I live by that I recorded from one of the books I read by a millionaire:

I am abundant in every good way

Infinite money is mine to earn, save, invest, exponentially multiply, and share

My abundant is making everyone better off

I embrace abundance and abundance embraces me

Notice the statement, *"My abundant is making everyone better off."* I believe this is the real secret to this entire affirmation being manifested in my life. Me, obtaining wealth is about blessing others. When you set yourself up to be a distribution center for the goodness of God to be seen throughout all the earth, then God will make sure you receive all that you need to achieve this goal. Sharing always creates more.

This is why I have to be extremely careful now what organization I join and invest my time in. I move in a different realm of productivity and manifestation than most people do. For example, I wrote this book in 72 hours and tweaked it another three or four days. Most things I do will be done from a supernatural favor realm.

Your level of giving and your financial competency about your giving will determine what measure you will experience in your life.

If I start something, it is like a back door opens to what I am doing and other blessings and unexpected advancements show up. Right now, I am in the midst of planning for a Book and Business Extravaganza Expo, which will be held within two months. In fact, I am releasing this book during the Expo. It has gotten the attention of Hollywood. One of the actors from a television series and movie called me personally wanting to host this event. When I hung up the phone with this actor, I said OMG – Oh, My God – my event has gotten the attention of Hollywood - talking about living in the overflow. But God wants to do the same in your life also.

Four Dimensions of Financial Release

It is in the book of Luke, Chapter 6 and verse 38 that we are introduced to this concept. It says that when we give, we can have an expectation to receive from four types of dimensions: good measure, pressed down, shaken together, and running over.

When the Bible was written it was written from an agricultural standpoint. In those days, farming was a reputable and common industry, so many of Jesus' parable and other scriptures often use metaphors that reflect farming contextual processes. This scripture in Luke is one of them.

It was talking about measuring grain in a basket to ensure full capacity was being reached. So this is what each of these measurements mean in regards to measuring grain.

- ❖ Good measure – The basket is full of grain

- ❖ Pressed down – Putting pressure on the grain in the basket so more can be added

- ❖ Shaken together – To make more compact to add more

- ❖ Running over – Basket becomes so full that it will overflow

The overflow is where God wants His people to live in. Don't settle for just the good measure, pressed down and shaken together. Press into the overflow.

Your level of giving and your financial competency about your giving will determine what measure you will experience in your life. Never allow anyone to derail you from believing God for His best for you. Your better days are ahead and it does not appear what you should be like. Keep pressing in no matter what. Remember, the day you decide to become wealthy and abundant, the universe will cheerfully provide.

YOU CAN SPEND YOUR DAYS

IN PROSPERITY!!!

Other Books By Dr. Shirley Clark

- ❖ The Midnight Cry
- ❖ Prayer, Push & Prevail
- ❖ The Ministry of Intercession
- ❖ Warring With Your Prophetic Word
- ❖ A Season of Purpose
- ❖ Intercessors' Insights
- ❖ Spiritual Warfare Teaching Manual and Workbook
- ❖ Prepare For War
- ❖ Personal Spiritual Warfare
- ❖ Strategic Warfare
- ❖ Empowering Your City
- ❖ The Power of the "IF" Prayer Manual
- ❖ 52 Laws of Prayer

Made in the USA
Columbia, SC
27 August 2020